The Development of the Violent Mind

The Case of Ted Bundy

I'm Not Guilty

Second Edition

Al Carlisle, Ph.D.

Encino, California

The Development of The Violent Mind
I'm Not Guilty: The Case of Ted Bundy

Copyright © 2013, 2014, 2016 Dr. Al Carlisle, Ph.D.

Edited by Dr. Michael R. Collings and Leya S. Booth

Published By:
Genius Book Publishing
PO Box 17752
Encino, CA 91416
www.GeniusBookPublishing.com

Follow us on Twitter: @GeniusBooks
Like us on Facebook: GeniusPublishing

ISBN: 978-0-9908575-6-3

Table of Contents

Part II: The Interview

I'M NOT GUILTY

The Case of Ted Bundy

Preface

From what we now know about Ted Bundy, it's puzzling how he could have walked among us, killing so many innocent victims without being detected for as long as he did. Even those who knew him best, such as co-workers in political campaigns, his girlfriend Elizabeth Kendall, and his family, didn't see him as he really was. Outwardly, he was articulate, friendly, intelligent, and had a winning smile. He expressed his concern for the poor and for minorities. He seemed to be an energetic, dedicated up-and-coming politician.

Ted Bundy was able to hide his destructive impulses from most people, but not from everyone.

During one of my first conversations with Ted, he asked me if I thought he had a multiple personality disorder. This question surprised me because it was completely out of context to what we had been discussing. I believe that Ted wanted to explore this question more fully, but couldn't. At the time, he was declaring his innocence of any crime and couldn't allow me to see the truth.

Ted was a very complex person. For the most part, people saw in him what Carl Jung referred to as a persona: a socially appropriate façade, a mask which obscured the sinister side of him. While Ted couldn't explain his dark side—Jung would have called it his Shadow—or where it originated, Ted knew it was a part of him. When this dark side was triggered into life, it took command of Ted's emotions and behavior. He argued with this side of him—whatever it was—but he couldn't stop it. And since he couldn't find a descriptive name for it, he gave it a sinister term, one which represented its mysterious nature and his fear of it. Ted called it the Entity.

My contact with Ted was at the Utah State Prison where I was employed as a psychologist working on the 90-Day evaluation unit. Ted had been convicted of the 1974 attempted abduction of Carol DaRonch. Judge Stewart Hanson, Jr., who had found Ted guilty of the crime, was left with the decision of how to sentence this promising University of Utah law student who appeared to have a bright future in politics. Would Judge Hanson give Ted prison time, or would he slap him on the wrist and put him on probation?

From what we know of Ted today, it's inconceivable that the option of probation could ever have been considered. We had before us one of the most violent serial killers in history and the judge was honestly considering the possibility of probation. In hindsight, the very idea of probation for Ted is unbelievable, and it underscores Ted's ability to present himself as a charming, respectable member of society.

Judge Hanson was a good judge, intelligent and fair. The consideration of probation was not due to inadequacy on his part. Instead, it was because of how Ted was viewed by those who knew him. Many felt that the police had caught the wrong man and that the court had mistakenly found him guilty of something he didn't do. Many felt that it would be an extreme travesty of justice to put this promising young man in prison. The judge had found him guilty, but due to the strong, conflicting opinions about Bundy's character, he requested psychological and psychiatric assessments to help him make a more informed decision. While Ted was on the 90-Day program, a mental health team including a psychiatrist, a social worker, and a psychologist—myself—evaluated him.

The first time I met Ted was in the hallway at the prison before our initial appointment. He walked briskly toward me with a smile on his face, and as he got close to me he extended his hand and gave me a strong handshake. He said, "Hi, I'm Ted Bundy. You must be Dr. Carlisle." His demeanor was more of a political candidate who was after my vote than of a killer who was facing a prison sentence.

The psychological evaluation of Ted Bundy was not easy. I conducted a lengthy series of interviews with Ted—over 20 hours all together—and also made telephone calls to people who knew him, both in the northwest and in Salt Lake City. This extended assessment was necessary due to the conflicting attitudes toward Ted. The combination of some findings from the psychological tests, the interview with Ted himself, and information I obtained from people who were close to him all convinced me that he had a violent dark side to him.

June 30, 1976 was the date of Ted Bundy's sentencing hearing. The psychiatric and psychological reports, along with the recommendations from the 90-Day program staff, had been sent to Judge Hanson and he had read them. Ted and his lawyer had also read the reports and they were poised to attack. I anticipated that I would be put on the stand to defend my report and I was very nervous about doing so because my conclusions were based on a combination of all of the findings I had obtained, and not from any one piece of evidence. The courtroom was crowded and it included Bundy's family, his girlfriend, the news media, law enforcement, and other interested or involved spectators.

Prior to the hearing, Judge Hanson had used the report's findings to make his decision. He already knew what sentence he wanted to impose on Ted, so he chose not to allow Ted's lawyer to put me on the stand. However, Ted was allowed to address the court.

Ted stood and faced the judge. Then he looked at me and began to angrily defend himself against conclusions from my report. He shook the report in the air and, with anger in his voice and tears in his eyes, declared that the report had been written to fit the crime and was totally inaccurate! He was so convincing that for a moment even I began to wonder if I had been too hard on him. Still, I had no doubt that my conclusions were correct.

Ted was sentenced to 1 to 15 years in the Utah State Prison. In spite of his bitterness in court, he contacted me at the prison and wanted to get together. Among other topics, he talked about his daily routine of exercising, reading inspirational books, and delving into his legal matters. He was quite friendly towards me. And when he escaped from jail the first time while in Colorado to face other charges, he called me just to chat.

Ted Bundy was, if nothing else, a study in contradictions. My intent in writing this book is to show Ted Bundy as he was: a conflicted, lonely, violent man who put so much effort into maintaining his persona that he lost track of himself altogether, allowing the Entity to grow within him. Over 30 women paid the price for Ted's loss of himself. I feel it is important to examine and understand the process through which a relatively normal, though troubled and shy, child could become such a violent killer. If nothing else, this book was written to answer the question "Why?"

I'm Not Guilty: The Case of Ted Bundy is the first of a series on the Development of the Violent Mind. The Bundy case is intriguing because it raised a number of questions regarding violence, and in particular serial killers.

Through in-depth interviews with other serial killers—Westley Alan Dodd, Keith Jesperson (Happy Face Killer), a Vietnam Marine who returned from the war and became a contract killer, and others, including, of course, Ted Bundy himself—I have come to a greater understanding of the development of a violent mind.

This book is divided into two parts. The first section begins with an explanation of what Ted calls the Entity, which is then followed by factual, evidence-based information about the life of Ted Bundy and how he became a serial killer.

The second section of the book takes our understanding of Ted Bundy one step further: it is a speculative interview along the lines of the interviews I had with him in 1976, wherein Ted and I discuss his experiences and the changes within him that turned him into a killer. This method has allowed me to explain how Bundy's personality most likely developed from childhood to become one of the most infamous serial killers of our time.

Prologue

Early in the evening of November 8, 1974, a man approached a small wooden building across the street from the Fashion Place Mall in Murray, Utah. He checked the business entrance and, when he found it locked, he also checked the side entrance. Satisfied that it too was locked, he turned and walked across the street towards the large shopping mall located at the corner of State Street and 61st South. His heart was beating rapidly and he wanted to run but he forced himself to walk at a normal rate to avoid calling attention to his actions. He paused at the entrance of the mall, turned, and looked back towards the parking lot. He was picky about his victims. Not too old, not too young, never fat. Always alone.

Eighteen-year-old Carol DaRonch had come to the mall to purchase a gift. She likely walked past this good-looking stranger without taking any notice of him. He had been watching her since she had left her car in the parking lot. She had not yet reached her destination when he called from behind her, "Excuse me, miss, do you own a Camaro, parked in the Sears section of the parking lot?"

"Yes," she said.

"I'm Officer Rosland of the Murray Police. A suspect has been detained trying to break into your car. If you would, I need you to come with me to your car to determine if anything is missing."

DaRonch later described him as young and good looking with a neatly trimmed mustache, and she detected nothing about him that would make her think that he was anything other than what he said he was.

When they reached her car there were no indications of a break-in. This "officer" told her the suspect must have been taken to the local substation and that she would have to accompany him there. He spoke with confidence and authority and, even though he was not dressed in police uniform, she had no reason to distrust him.

He led her over to the other side of the mall to a small wooden building across the street, telling her that it was a police substation. It was locked. She would have to accompany him to the local police department and, pointing to his Volkswagen, instructed her to get in. Something did not feel right but she climbed in.

He started the engine and then turned to look at her. His appearance immediately changed from the kind young man who was trying to help her to something evil. He slapped handcuffs on her but in the struggle he inadvertently got both cuffs on one wrist. She screamed and struggled to fight him off but he was too quick. Too powerful. He reached across her to lock her door but failed. He picked up a bar to strike her but she was already throwing herself out of the car. Another automobile was coming up from behind him, so he made a quick U-turn and headed back the other way. An elderly couple was shocked by the image of a frantic girl with handcuffs on one wrist, screaming on the side of the road.

Nobody got a license plate number.

Later that evening, a drama production was taking place at Viewmont High School in Bountiful, Utah, a town located just north of Salt Lake. A man with a cast on his arm was seen standing in the hall attempting to balance a number of books, stopping female students, asking them to help him get his books to his car. Nobody paused to help him. Debbie Kent, a local high school student, had come with her parents to watch the production. She excused herself during the intermission to go pick up her brother. She was never seen again. The man was later seen sitting at the back of the auditorium during the production.

Eight months later, Sgt. Bob Hayward of the Utah Highway Patrol was watching late at night for speeders in a Westside neighborhood. He became suspicious when a Volkswagen drove past with its lights out. Hayward switched on his flashing lights and pulled behind the Volkswagen, causing the frightened driver to run a stop sign. Hayward stopped him and, in the process of searching his vehicle, found a set of handcuffs, a ski mask, some rope, and an ice pick. Hayward also noticed that the passenger seat was missing. It looked as if these items might be burglary tools so the driver was arrested. The driver identified himself as Ted Bundy, a student at the University of Utah Law School. The handcuffs in Bundy's car later connected him with the DaRonch case several months earlier.

At this same time, authorities from Seattle were asking the Salt Lake Sheriff's Office to check on Ted Bundy, a person of interest in a series of homicides in the state of Washington. Bundy was investigated, tried, and found guilty of Attempted Kidnap on Carol DaRonch, and was then sent to the Utah State Prison for the 90-Day evaluation.

I was intrigued by the Bundy phenomenon. Ann Rule, a popular non-fiction true crime writer, manned a crisis line with him in Seattle and found him to be sensitive and caring. However, journalists Stephen Michaud and Hugh Aynesworth wrote about the monster in him in their excellent book, *The Only Living Witness*. A wife of a prominent leader in Salt Lake was so impressed with Ted Bundy that she had hopes that he would become her son-in-law. Ted expressed a desire to be baptized into the Church of Jesus Christ of Latter-day Saints and took the time to go through the missionary discussions. Two Mormon missionaries and a Mormon Bishop who witnessed his conversion were convinced that it was genuine.

Prior to Bundy's execution, he met a number of times with religious leaders, including Dr. James Dobson, head of the Christian evangelical organization Focus on the Family. Ted said that pornography was a significant part of why he became a serial killer. These religious professionals, who also had considerable experience with criminal populations, expressed a belief that Ted had repented of his sins. After years of adamantly professing his innocence, he confessed his crimes to Dr. Bob Keppel, a retired detective who had headed up the investigations on him in Seattle.

Ted Bundy is as much of an enigma today as he was when he was alive. Can pornography create a serial killer? Can a person kill dozens of women and then "repent"' of his acts? Can a killer such as Ted Bundy ever really *feel* regret for such brutal homicides?

What information could have been obtained from Ted Bundy, had he been willing to open himself up to one more interview before his execution? Had he, under this circumstance, been willing to open up, we would know much more about the process of how a person becomes a serial killer.

The importance of studying Ted Bundy's life is not simply to more fully understand Ted Bundy; it is to shed light on how an ordinary child coming from an ordinary family and having a normal education can become a killer. Perhaps any given child not only has the capability of achieving great things in life in sports, art, music, or education, but can also condition himself to feel justified in killing innocent victims. It may be that we are not only capable of becoming angels; we are also capable of enjoying vicious destruction of human life.

Serial killers do not grow up thinking they would like a life of killing people. When they kill their first victim, they are generally alarmed and surprised and say they do not understand how it could have happened. Arthur Gary Bishop was executed for the deaths of five boys in Salt Lake. On my first visit with him on Death Row at the Utah State Prison, he said, "I'm ready to die for my crimes but I first want to understand how I got to the point that I could kill another person and why I continued doing so after I had killed my first victim."

Part I: The Creation of a Serial Killer

The Entity

When Ted Bundy was arrested and tried for homicide in Florida, he spoke of an uncontrollable violent process within him. He called this process, this combination of emotions and behaviors, an Entity. He wasn't implying that he had a multiple personality disorder, but he did indicate to Dr. Dorothy Lewis, a psychiatrist from New York who conducted a psychiatric assessment on him, that this process, or "thing" within him was as if he had another personality and that this entity would take over his functioning and allow or cause him to commit a homicide.

> D.L.: Did you ever have a sense of another Ted, or another person? Did you ever actually talk to the other?
>
> T.B.: Oh, yes. In fact—oh, yes—I'd have this dialogue.

D.L.: I don't mean thinking, "Gee, you're nuts to do this." I mean, did you ever feel like another person?

T.B.: It reached a point, I would say in '74, where . . . it would have conversations. And I'm not saying that I was a multiple personality. I don't know. All I know is that this other part of myself seemed to have a voice and seemed to have a need.

D.L.: What was the voice like?

T.B.: It was . . . I can sort of remember it was just very low, kind of cruel and demanding.

D.L.: What would it say?

T.B.: Oh, it would walk down the street . . .

D.L.: Pardon?

T.B. I'd walk down the street and literally hear it talking about women I'd seen.

D.L.: What would it say?

T.B.: Oh, it had this category . . . system of categorizing young women, you know, I can't, I used to, it's been so long since that I can't remember.

D.L.: It's very, very important to understand how this evolved, the voice.

T.B.: Well, it seemed, the more, especially in '74 particularly, the more deeply I got into this, the stronger, the more dominant and strong this voice became. I felt captive of this whole part of myself.

D.L.: When did it talk to you?

T.B.: Most clearly when I was very aroused. And certainly when I was intoxicated.

D.L.: Then you would hear it.

T.B.: Yes.

D.L.: Did it ever frighten you?

T.B.: When it frightened me it scared me to death and made me just cry out to stop.

D.L.: You would?

T.B.: Oh, yes. Like the next day after something happened. After the first time, I felt like a captive. I felt . . . I can't . . . I felt like, up till that point, I said, "Okay, you haven't gone too far yet. It's okay. You're going to stop now." And I'd stop . . . and then all of a sudden, it'd be back. The day after the first time this happened I was in a panic. In hysteria and fear and sorrow and horror over what had happened and said, "What in God's name has, have I done here?" . . . Then I found myself to have become, more or less, a hostage.

D.L.: It sounds as if you feel you then became that voice.

T.B.: Well, yeah. More or less, it takes over the whole, it takes over the basic consciousness mechanism and more or less dictates what's going to be done.

D.L.: It says, like "Now you're going to do . . . ?"

T.B.: Dictates just like you would dictate to yourself that you are going to do something, you know.

D.L.: Have you ever been told that you did something you didn't remember? The reason I'm asking is that I am wondering, because you raised the issue of multiple personality, to what extent are you, who I'm talking with now, really separate from the other entity and to what extent it's just a variant of a mood you get.

T.B.: Yeah. I hear what you're saying. I think that there's more, an integration there, an inter-relationship, which when the malignant portion of my personality or consciousness, call it what you will—the entity—is more or less directing the mood and the action. I'm still on another level conscious of this, I'm not totally unconscious or, or unaware of it.

D.L.: It's just that you're in a slightly altered state.

T.B.: It could certainly be another way of describing it. I'm not saying this certainly isn't a strictly alternate personality.

D.L.: You've said that later, after the entity became stronger, it did seem to have a voice.

T.B: Yes. It seemed to have a sense, a voice, just like a poem has a voice or a book had a voice.

D.L.: But did you actually talk back to your voice?

T.B.:   Right. And there would be times, distinct, so distinct that a dialogue was really, you know, happening.

D.L.:   You couldn't shut it off?

T.B.:   No.

D.L.:   Did you ever tell it to shut the hell up?

T.B.:   Oh yes. It wouldn't. It just wouldn't stop.[1]

There were no indications that Ted had schizophrenia. He was not psychotic to the point that he couldn't differentiate between fantasy/delusions and reality. He mentioned that a force within him "call it what you will—the entity—is more or less directing the mood and the action."

Developmental Profile of Ted Bundy

Not all serial killers are the same as Ted Bundy. In an interview I had with Keith Jesperson, the Happy Face Killer, there were no indications that he dissociated into fantasy before or during a homicide. Neither did two serial child sexual killers in my research, Arthur Gary Bishop and Westley Allan Dodd. Not all serial killers kill a victim while living a fantasy. However, I believe that some do, and Ted Bundy was likely one of them. Fantasy dissociation in general and dissociation during a violent crime, including dissociation during a homicide, are not uncommon.

In an article I wrote some years ago, *The Divided Self: Towards an Understanding of the Dark Side of the Serial Killer*, I indicated how fantasy and dissociation can become linked together in a powerful way. My conclusions were as follows:

Dissociation and the Separate Self

The concept of an altered self, or altered identity, has its scientific roots in the findings of such persons as Sigmund Freud, Carl Jung, Pierre Janet, and Josef Breuer. Freud postulated that there was a subconscious mind, a "hidden" level of consciousness generally not accessible to the conscious processes. He demonstrated fairly conclusively that traumatic memories and emotions from a person's past could be housed in the subconscious which could later have a strong effect on their emotional life and behavior. Freud and Breuer found a connection between behavioral symptoms and subconscious memories which they referred to as a "splitting of consciousness" or dual consciousness processes.

Ernest Hilgard comments regarding simultaneous, dual levels of thinking:

> Even more intriguing and puzzling is the possibility that in some instances part of the attentive effort and planning [in which a person may engage] may continue without any awareness of it at all. When that appears to be the case, the concealed part of the total ongoing thought and action may be described as *dissociated* from the conscious experience of the person.[2]

The Role of Fantasy

While in the usual case of dissociation traumatic memories are buried, allowing the person to avoid experiencing the pain, on the opposite side of the coin is the process of creating fantasy imagery, or illusions, for the purpose of avoiding pain and generating excitement. Walter Young found that a traumatized child who became Multiple Personality Disorder (MPD) would incorporate fantasy imagery into a personality identity. In the same manner, a child who experiences excessive emptiness and engages in extensive daydreaming may reach the point where the identity or process generated through the fantasy becomes a compartmentalized and controlling factor in the person's life.

A fantasy is an imagery process in which a person attempts to obtain vicarious gratification by engaging in acts in his mind which he currently is not able to do (or doesn't dare do) in reality. Fantasy is a mechanism by which a temperament, such as anger, can begin to take on form with a specified purpose and direction. Ongoing and intense fantasy is also a mechanism by which hate and bitterness can begin to become dissociated and compartmentalized from the more ethically focused aspects of the mind. Intensely painful memories and deep emptiness can lead to vivid fantasies, which over time can take on a greater and greater degree of reality.

When a person is intensely absorbed in a fantasy, he dissociates from everything around him. Anger and emptiness become the energy and motivating forces behind the fantasy. While actively engaged in the fantasy the person experiences a sense of excitement and relief. However, when it is over there is still a feeling of emptiness because the fantasy has whetted an appetite for the real thing, which he anticipates will be even more enjoyable than the fantasy. Thus, through fantasy, the person creates a make-believe world wherein he can accomplish what he cannot do in reality. Over time, the person may turn to this pseudo-existence with increasing rapidity when he feels stress, depression, or emptiness. This can result in a dual identity, one part being that associated with reality and the people he comes in contact with every day (Carl Jung's Persona), and the other part the secret identity through which he is able to manifest the power and control he would like over others (Carl Jung's Shadow concept). If the person is angry and bitter, this alter-identity becomes an image of destruction. The major problem is that heavy fantasy is inexorably linked to the process of dissociation and compartmentalization. As the person shifts back and forth between the two identities in his attempt to meet his needs they both become an equal part of him, the opposing force being suppressed when he is attempting to have his needs met through the one. Over time, the dark side (representing the identity or "entity" the person has created to satisfy his deepest hunger) becomes stronger than the "good" side, and the person begins to experience being possessed, or controlled by this dark side of him. This is partly because the dark side is the part anticipated to meet the person's strongest needs, and partly because the good side is the part which experiences the guilt for the "evil" thoughts, and therefore out of necessity is routinely suppressed. Thus, the monster is created. Bill (pseudo name), a person who became a multiple homicide offender, describes the need he had for fantasy as a child:

> I think that anybody who would look upon me, at least for the first hour after reading the book would think I was preoccupied . . . With most people when they put the book down they are back to the real world . . . whereas in my case, these would provide scenarios that I would yearn for, and wish could happen. I was in there [inside the story]. I could almost smell the smells, see the sights. I was gone. I was in another world.[3]

Stephen G. Michaud and Hugh Aynesworth interviewed Ted Bundy for several months. They asked him to give them his impressions about the serial killer who had killed the women in the Northwest, Utah, and Colorado. It was a brilliant technique and it worked. Ted Bundy, in telling how a psychopathic killer is created, stated:

> There is some kind of weakness that gives rise to this individual's interest in the kind of sexual activity involving violence that would gradually begin to absorb some of his fantasy . . . eventually the interest would become so demanding toward new material that it could only be catered to by what he could find in the dirty book stores . . . [4]

As this process continues, it begins to dominate his life. Bundy continues:

> By peeping in windows, as it were, and watching a woman undress, or watching whatever could be seen, you know, during the evening, and approaching it almost like a project, throwing himself into it, uh, literally for years . . . He gained, you'd say, a terrific amount of . . . at times . . . a great amount of gratification from it and he became increasingly adept at it as anyone becomes adept at anything they do over and over and over again . . . and as the condition develops and its purposes or characteristics become more well defined, it begins to demand more of the attention and time of the individual . . . there is a certain amount of tension, uh, struggle between the normal personality and this, this, uh, psychopathological, uh, entity. [5]

Eventually it can get out of control. Bundy added:

> Well, we, we . . . ah, described this individual and found that his behavior, which was becoming more and more frequent, was also *concomitantly* . . . occupying more and more of his mental and intellectual energies. So he's facing a greater, ah, more frequent *challenge* of this darker side of himself to his normal life.[6]

Bob, one of the homicide offenders in my research, described the power of the dark side when he considered killing a victim:

> The beast can take over to complete an identity if you leave a hole in yourself. In other words, it seeks a vacuum. In a healthy person the vacuum doesn't exist. There's a sense of identity that prevents a need for the dark awareness.
>
> It was very much like there was a battlefield in my head, wrestling with what I as a human being felt to be reasonable alternatives. It was a battle between two very different parts of myself—goodness and evil. When you feel evil, there is a sense of power. It can consume you. There is not much intellect involved in making an evil decision. It's a more gripping thing, more animalistic. It's so much simpler and so much easier to give into it than to hang on to a moral structure that you don't understand, or an ethic or value or commitment, all the things that make us human beings.[7]

Bob tried to control the thoughts and images regarding the killing of his victim:

> I just kept trying to shake it off and physically I would shake my head to rid myself of the thoughts. I wondered where they could come from, or without my pulse going, how I could consider such an ugly sequence of events.[8]

When this didn't work, he attempted to indulge in the fantasy rather than fight it to see if that would work. He continued:

> Let's give in to the thoughts. Let's not try to resist it. Let's grovel in it for maybe 20 minutes. Maybe that will dissipate it. Maybe it will blow off some steam. Let's have a fantasy, Okay? What happened was, I became preoccupied with the fantasy. It did not resolve itself.[9]

When Bob felt he couldn't fight the homicidal impulses any longer he decided to go with the plan and to kill his victim. When he began planning the homicide,

> my mouth would dry up, my peripheral vision would narrow, and I would be at peace. This was a plan that [at] whatever cost would accomplish what I wanted and would create balance in my life. There is a sweetness in surrendering to any plan. To allow yourself to commit to a plan provides a platform in your life where you're not at drift . . . Here there is power. Here there is meaning, logic and order

and stability. If I have to give in to an evil thing to do it, it is worth it.[10]

None of these people I have mentioned have been diagnosed with a Dissociative Identity Disorder (previously called a Multiple Personality Disorder). They were all aware to one degree or another of what they were doing when they selected and killed their victims. The primary point is that dissociated violent fantasy can become a powerful controlling factor in a person's life.

I asked an inmate we will call Bill, who is in prison on a multiple homicide charge, to send me a letter regarding his interpretation of what Ted Bundy called the Entity. He wrote the following:

> If a compulsion is a powerful urge or impulse so irresistible that it simply overwhelms an individual's will to fight it off, then it's perfectly understandable why Ted Bundy would see an Entity as the driving force compelling him, at times against his will, to abduct and murder women. This is not to suggest that he was the victim of some supernatural possession, demonic or otherwise. And, if I remember correctly, Bundy himself never claimed such to be the case. But, while he was probably trying to deflect blame and responsibility from himself by speaking of this Entity, I don't think he should be branded a liar for suggesting that, at times, he *felt* as if he was being driven to violence by something or someone other than himself.

The fact of the matter is that *no one,* not even someone as reviled as Ted Bundy, is born with an inherent desire to inflict harm upon others. If a youngster's psyche is so wounded or battered that his first taste of imaginary violence provides him with a profound sense of psychological restoration, then his conscience will need to be convinced that it's okay to continue thinking such thoughts. And it is the tension of this inner conflict–knowing that such thoughts are *not* right, but needing the psychological relief that this imaginary violence provides–that gives rise to the sense of an Entity pulling the individual in opposite directions within his conscience.

In my own case, I never heard any voices or felt any unseen supernatural presence when I was first exposed to (and tantalized by) violent pornography. But, because this sadistic imagery fed and restored my psyche right from the beginning, there immediately arose that aforementioned tension, a seeming clash of wills inside my conscience. And from that point onward, whenever I dabbled with hurting someone in my imagination, there was something inside of me that said, "This is *wrong.*" This, of course, was my conscience conveying to me its moral sense of right and wrong. But, at the same time, there was also a discernible impression that competed within and against my conscience, conveying the message that "It's *okay* to think such thoughts. Girls don't like you.

They don't want you. So why not imagine hurting them in your mind? It not only feels good, but it's fair! So, go ahead. It's okay."

Again, I never actually heard those words verbalized out loud. But, even though I was the one who chose to continue fantasizing sadistic violence for the restorative pleasure it provided me, I nevertheless often felt myself being urged on to do so by "some form of something," as Bundy called it, that wordlessly but powerfully impressed upon me the notion: "you *need* this!" Did I ever personify any of this, in real time, by suggesting the presence of a malevolent "Entity" that was controlling my behavior? No, I did not. But, if you had suggested to me such a thing *back then*, when I was an 11- or 12-year old kid who was regularly brutalizing his female classmates in his imagination, my thoughtful considered response might well have been, "Yeah…it certainly does *feel* like some Entity is controlling me."

Such is the power of a full-blown compulsion that it takes on a life of its own, giving it the Entity-like, evil-personified quality to which Ted Bundy alluded. Indeed, it is the Entity-like quality of a full-blown compulsion that explains why Bundy could say…"I'm just like everyone else." (By which he meant, "Aside from the fact that I'm driven by some evil unseen Entity to rape and murder college coeds, I'm just as normal as any other red-blooded American male.")

How could he possibly have believed such a thing? Because compulsions *always* give rise to desperation, and desperation *always* feels as if it's being forced upon the individual by something or someone *outside* one's own self. Especially after a string of unsuccessful abduction attempts, Ted Bundy *must* have felt maddenly desperate, as if seized and held captive by the murderous impulses that set out on a hunt in the first place. And this desperation would have made it seem all the more real to him that something or someone other than himself was compelling him to act out.

Even when I felt euphorically and deliriously well-sated by acting out violence, I've also experienced a troubling sense of having rubbed elbows with pure evil–as if my violence wasn't really *by* me or *for* me. This, of course, was only my compulsion speaking, deluding me in such a way as to minimize my actions and my culpability. But, from personal experience, I *do* understand how Ted Bundy could actually feel that at least some of his crimes were committed less for himself than for his "Entity."[11]

If a person allows it to get out of control it can result in a homicide, and at times in multiple homicides.

The Vulnerability Stage

A serial killer generally has experienced trauma in his early childhood which makes him vulnerable for some type of pathology. The traumas are the usual ones which are common for most children. It is not the traumas which create the killer. It's the manner in which he responds to them.

Ted was born on November 24, 1946. World War II had ended a year before and the country was beginning to rebuild itself following years of depression and poverty. Louise Cowell was living in Philadelphia with her parents at the time. She got pregnant. We don't know for sure who the father was or whether or not very many people knew she was pregnant. Sex outside of marriage was a severe breach of moral conduct and an illegitimate pregnancy was a humiliation for the entire family. An abortion was unthinkable. A couple of months before her child was to be born a decision was made that she should not have the child in Philadelphia. Louise went to the Elizabeth Lund Home for Unwed Mothers in Burlington, Vermont, where she had her child and then they returned home to Philadelphia. Her child was named Theodore Robert Cowell.

Ted began his life as a typical child. He wasn't aware that he was conceived by an unknown father or that he was born in a foundling home. However, he was born at a time in history in which if he were to later learn the true facts of his birth it could (and did) have a major effect on his life.

Ted spent the first two years of his childhood with his grandparents, reportedly believing that his mother was his sister and that his grandparents were his parents. It's unclear, however, if Ted actually thought his mother was his sister or if that was a story the family told to others to hide his illegitimacy. There is no evidence that this belief about his mother being his sister was a major issue when he was a child.

There are stories about his grandfather having a violent temper but there are other stories about how Ted loved his grandfather. There are a couple of stories about Ted showing some violent tendencies when he was a small child prior to moving to the Northwest. However, there isn't enough consistency in the stories to affirm their truth.

Shortly before Ted's fourth birthday, he and his mother were invited to go to Tacoma, Washington where Louise's uncle and family were living. The move was difficult for Ted and he didn't seem to adjust easily to the rapid changes in his life. Louise got a job as a secretary at the Council of Churches and then she met John Culpepper Bundy at a gathering at the First Methodist Church. Louise and John soon married and Ted became Ted Bundy. Ted was close to his mother when he was young but he had little respect for his stepfather. As other children came into the home, he was in the difficult position of being the oldest child, yet a stepson. He had lost the emotional contact with his grandparents and now he was required to share his mother with a stepfather and younger siblings. He had a sister Linda born in 1952, a brother Glenn in 1954, followed by another sister Sandra in 1956, and then another brother Richard in 1961. He was closest to Richard.

His life at that time consisted of family, school, and association with kids in his neighborhood. Media entertainment came from the radio. He enjoyed spending evenings outside talking to friends in his neighborhood. He wasn't abused by his parents and he and others described his parents as God-fearing people. He was raised in a conservative religious family with a strong work ethic. Ted was also active in his church.

Ted wasn't a leader among his friends; he was more passive than active. A woman I spoke with who grew up with him from his neighborhood said Ted wasn't rebellious or oppositional and he demonstrated no noticeable characteristics of anger or violence. He was the nice kid who was, as she saw it, "just . . . there, that's all, just there."[12] He didn't call attention to himself. As far as she was concerned, he was a normal boy in all respects. He did have two good friends from his neighborhood who continued to be close to him throughout his teenage years, Terry Storwick and Warren Dodge.

He was very sensitive about being poor in an upper-middle class school. He had a strong desire to achieve and said he was humiliated when he wasn't in the top spelling circle in the 4th grade.

Ted was a troubled child. However, this doesn't mean that he would grow up to kill people. The specific trauma in a child's life is not as important a factor leading to a violent personality as is the manner in which the child reacts to it.

Beginning of Fantasy

As a child, Ted was interested in the weekly serials on the radio. This was common to almost all children in those days. Some children also develop strong individual interests in sports, art, music, or academics. Ted wasn't good in any of these areas. He did develop an early interest in political activities, which is unique for any child. His uncle was a hero figure to him because he was intelligent and he was a professor at a university. Ted wanted to be like him, and even took up his uncle's interest in classical music.

Like many children, Ted found great comfort in his fantasy activities. Young children take the part of the hero, both in their interactive play with each other and also in their daydreams. The weekly serials and the political speeches that fascinated him gave him ample opportunity to fashion a winning personality, even if it was only in his daydreams. Ted went a step beyond simply daydreaming; he sat up late at night on his bed with his earphones on, memorizing parts of political speeches he heard on his small crystal radio. His need to be great like the politicians he listened to was very strong.

Preteens and Sex

A sexual awakening is a normal process in the life of most boys. In most cases it leads to healthy social interactions, dating, and enjoyable—albeit sometimes traumatic—interpersonal activities. If sex becomes a powerful escape from loneliness, it can have dramatic consequences.

Ted completed elementary school and advanced into junior high school. He told me that he dated a few times and even began kissing and sexually touching a girl, and said he enjoyed it, as did the girl. Then it stopped. When I asked him why this normal social activity didn't continue, he said, "Gee Al, I don't know what it could have been." I felt strongly that something did happen but Ted didn't want to talk about it and, as far as I'm aware, Ted never reported to anyone about being hurt by a girl at this age. Still, it must have been something significant since he didn't go on another date until his senior year in high school.

It is not uncommon for a boy to discover sex when he is in his early teens. For most boys it's a rite of passage although not a change that invariably controls a young boy's life. However, Ted found that his friends from his neighborhood were expanding their lives into school activities. When Ted tried it, it didn't work for him. He tried football but he was too small. He tried running for a school office but was unsuccessful. He wasn't confident in his social skills so, when his friends got into outside-the-neighborhood activities, he stayed home.

Ted felt left out. He was even more alone now. He would often go out at night and spend time with the kids in the neighborhood, but when he entered high school they were around less and less because of other activities in which they were involved.

Under conditions such as this, a young boy finds comfort wherever he can. Ted had already discovered the importance of fantasy in his life.

Bill (previously cited), a killer of multiple victims, reported to me the importance of fantasy in a child's life:

> I think the fantasy life leaned toward making me feel good because I think that everybody vicariously lives what they are reading. The difference is that with most people when they do put the book down they are back to the real world and they know they are not that [person they were fantasizing about]. Whereas, in my case, these would provide scenarios that I would yearn for and wish could happen, that I could be this hero. In terms of actually being in the story, I think that anybody who would look

upon me, at least for the first hour after reading the book, would think I was preoccupied. I was still in it for that period of time.[13]

Bill related how it affected him when he found masturbation:

My life was transformed from that day on. My thoughts were consumed with what had happened. It's as if I had tasted heaven and I wanted to be nowhere else but there. And so, at school, that's the only thing I could think of. It became an everyday thing. I mean that literally. I don't think a day passed in the next three or four years that I didn't engage in masturbation.

That behavior became my means of dealing with any kind of crisis, any kind of bad feelings I may have had. All I had to do was go back to imagination, masturbate and I'd feel good and the crisis wasn't so bad. That became not just a means but the only means. So that by the time my interest in girls like that of any boy that age came to be, when I felt rejected, I could retreat to my sexual fantasies.[14]

Then Ted discovered autoerotic sex. Masturbation was a serious taboo which parents and religions severely warned against. Now Ted had a problem. He could either give up an activity which he had found to be a very enjoyable adventure, or he could keep doing it and hide it from others. Sexual fantasy with masturbation and then later window peeking at night gave life to him and there was no way that he was going to let it go.

How then would he handle the guilt? It could be strong at first but a person can learn to shut it out. With practice it can become easier and easier over time. It wasn't that he had the inability to feel guilt, it's that he learned to justify what he was doing.

Bill added:

> Having withdrawn into this world, there was nothing there to act as a deterrent. I played with other kids but I didn't have any real friends. When we finished playing I would retreat into my own little world and that blocked out anything. I saw myself as different but not abnormal.[15]

Ted justified it to me by saying, "I was not apprehensive towards establishing new relationships. I was just as secure with academic life. Social relations were not important." That was not true.

Mid-Teens: The Waiting Game

The teenage years are a time when a boy begins to broaden his social activities. He attempts to find his niche within his group. If he can do so, deeper pathology can be averted.

Ted felt inadequate and couldn't reach out to establish himself. Throughout high school he struggled with loneliness and not fitting in. He was viewed as intelligent and as having a sense of humor, but he was very shy. He was painfully aware that something was missing in his life, or in him, but he was unable to find a way to change it. One event which caused a serious problem in his life was learning from his cousin that he was illegitimate. He later told two women that he felt that no one would want to marry him because of this. Ted never did get over that and he was angry at his mother for years for not telling him.

The day before his execution Ted told Dr. Dobson of Focus on the Family that he was getting heavily involved with window peeking and pornography throughout his junior high and high school years. He blamed pornography and crime magazines as primary causal factors that resulted in him becoming a serial killer. A sexual appetite was beginning to develop fairly early in his life.

He got involved with student political activities on campus during his senior and possibly his junior year in high school. He campaigned for his friends who were running for student office and began to discover a niche that would work for him. He would continue to work on political campaigns in the future. This was a strong area of success for him.

Ted didn't have a car during his high school years but a couple of his friends invited him to go skiing with them. He forged ski tickets by changing the date stamped on the ticket. This, along with his campaigning, allowed him for a short while to be "one of the boys." Now for the first time he felt what it was like to be accepted by the elite. It was a very powerful experience. However, it was also one of his most painful. He had full acceptance by his friends when he was skiing but, when they got home, he again found he was not wanted. They went to dances or other activities following the ski trips and Ted went home—alone.

At this point in his life, Ted was lonely, he was immature, and he was poor. However, he was intelligent and he had political skills. Under the right circumstances he could find the success he so desperately craved. He believed he could find it through a political career and a beautiful wife who could be an asset to him in his career. A combination of the two could give him wealth and status and he would never have to be a poor second-class person again. Other than his shyness, his biggest problem at this point was his sexual activities. His pornography, voyeurism, and his crime magazines were his primary means of escape from depression and loneliness.

His goal was to represent the USA in reestablishing a relationship with China. He was determined that he wouldn't remain poor. He would have expensive clothes, status, and a beautiful and intelligent girlfriend, which would all come once he got into college.

There is one additional event that would have had an extremely strong impact on his life if, in point of fact, it happened. A young girl who lived close to Ted disappeared and was never seen again. Ted had a paper route in her area and some people believe that he talked her into coming out of her house during the night and then he molested and killed her. Other people believe that he was not the one who killed the girl. This issue has never been resolved.

Shattering of the Dream

When an empty and lonely person rigidly puts all of his hopes into a single dream, there is a sense of urgency and desperation. He rushes into it. However, there is a loss of flexibility, a loss of spontaneity. The first deep romance can be overwhelmingly wonderful to a love-starved boy.

Ted graduated from Wilson High School in 1965 with a B average. He enrolled at the University of Puget Sound (UPS) which was not his first choice; his few friends were going to other universities. He enrolled at UPS because he had no car. He could live at home and commute, which would allow him and his family to save money on his education. It was a frustrating disappointment for him because the students were heavily involved with fraternity and sorority activities, and he didn't have the money to get into a fraternity. That was an unhappy year for him.

He completed his freshman year at UPS and got involved with some political activities during the summer, which gave him a taste of greater possibilities to come. He transferred to the University of Washington for his sophomore year. He was becoming more opinionated and would take the sides of the Blacks in the Watts riots. He felt the People's Republic of China was treated unjustly by the United States. His goal was to obtain an academic position with the State Department and to work on Mainland China in trade. He said, "I wanted to gain a position of authority to improve relations with China." His goals were admirable.

He met an Asian girl and they began dating. However, her family convinced her that she and Ted were of different cultures and a long-term relationship wouldn't work out. Ted was not devastated by this failure; he had tested the waters and had discovered that a girl would go out with him. After her positive response to him he had more confidence that there would be others.

Then it happened—his dream girl walked into his life. He met Marjorie one weekend while skiing and quickly fell in love with her. She was everything he had dreamed of. She was beautiful. She had poise and grace. She had even engaged in some modeling. She was career-oriented and had a solid work ethic.

And, most of all, she was attracted to him.

He sold himself to her with stories of future greatness. His goals were genuine and possibly reachable, and this impressed her. However, beneath the beautifully painted surface there was a boy who felt inferior and inadequate, and there was only a thin shell which separated the dark interior from the superficial exterior of his personality. He played the role of the person he aspired to be. It was fake but it showed promise. However, sooner or later she would begin to get to know the real Ted.

Bill, the killer I referred to previously, talked about the powerful need an extremely lonely person has for love:

> Whenever a person is driven by strong anxiety and psychic exhaustion, the result is necessarily a loss of spontaneity and flexibility. To a neurotic, the gaining of affection is not a luxury, nor primarily a source of strength or pleasure but a vital necessity. The difference is one between I wish and enjoy being loved and I must be loved at any cost. Or the difference between someone who eats because he enjoys his appetite and can be discriminating about his food and another person who is near starvation and must take food indiscriminately and will pay any price for it.[16]

Initially, the relationship with Marjorie worked and Ted's social confidence began to grow. This was the second girl who had taken an interest in him and it appeared as if this one could go all the way. Ted found a car he could afford, he was doing well in college, and he even had a girlfriend who cared for him. This was possibly the happiest time of his life and he anticipated that it would continue. The problem was that he was like a used car salesman who was trying to make a customer believe that an inferior product (himself) was a wonderful car. It worked for over a year.

There was a lady who knew Ted fairly well during the time he was going with Marjorie. She worked with him in his employment and helped him find a job. In a phone conversation she reported the following:

I'm a woman 70 years old and I know what goes on but he doesn't have it.

[What was he like when you first met him?]

I don't know if he was high on dope or liqueur, but he was sure a peculiar person.

[What would he do?]

He was going with a girl from San Francisco. He would portray himself to be a really big politician to try to get in good with her family. He sometimes used a British accent. He borrowed Havilland China and sterling silver and linen from me and had her there for dinner and he was going to show her what a fine cook he was, and what a man he would be around the house. He got her drunk and they spent the night there.

He borrowed my car several times to go out on night trips. I was scared to death when he was gone. Something was up because he just wasn't running true to form of where he was going or what he was doing.

He got him a job at the Olympic Hotel and went through the men's employee lockers and found some old tuxedo waiter's clothes (pants, coat, etc.). He got them fixed up and would dress himself up as if he were the head waiter in some restaurant. He lived for a short while with an elderly couple and they were going to go to Norway. They finally had to ask him to move.

I helped him get a job at Safeway for a short while and he just quit, not even going back to work to tell them he was leaving.

He borrowed $100.00 from me. I tried to get it back but he always had some reason why he couldn't pay me back right then. He never did pay me back. I talked to his mother once and asked her if she would appeal to him as a man to return the $100.00 I loaned to him. His mother said, "He doesn't live here anymore and we're not responsible for anything he does."

He is a very, very peculiar boy. He was just kind of sneaking around. He'd be on the telephone when you'd least expect him to be. He would tell you he was going to be one place and he would be somewhere else. He left the city on a plane and he said he was going to Colorado to be a ski instructor there. Something happened and he came back.

He went to Pennsylvania and drove his uncle's Cadillac and came back flat broke looking for a job. All in all, he's just a very weird boy.

I worked with him at the Seattle Yacht Club when he was a busboy and I got him a job at the Olympic Hotel. Then he got a job at Safeway. Then he got into politics and I called and told [his supervisors] he was a strange boy and a little on the crooked side.

He was six weeks at the Yacht Club and they let him go. He wasn't supposed to eat the food, but he was always in the pantry eating all the fresh foods and whipped cream he could get and all the fancy foods he could eat. He would grab them and take them to his locker.

[Did he ever seem a close person to get next to, or was he distant?]

He had kind of a running game of his own. He didn't have too much to do with his family. He borrowed my car a couple of times saying he was going home. Ted never talked about his family or showed much affection for them. He spent quite a bit of time at a friend's house, an antique dealer who had been in prison and this guy went back at least once after Ted knew him.

Ted told me he was studying Chinese at the U. of Washington. When the draft seemed to get close he told me he was going to skip out and go to Taiwan.

I have been suspicious from the day those two girls were killed at Lake Sammamish with that "Ted." I remember him seeing him in an Albertson's store in Green Lake with a cast on his arm. I was going to do something about it, but living alone I was afraid to do more than what I had already done.

[Did he seem strange? Mentally ill or a criminal?]

He seemed to have mental problems. He had ways of getting money. He had a very expensive overcoat with a fur collar that came from the Yankee Peddler, one of the men's best dress shops in the University District. He had a key to the men's dormitory at the University of Washington long after he was no longer a student there. He carried the key with him and used to go in there and sleep on the lounge couches when he didn't have any place to go and he would take clothing and things from the dorm.

I was willing to give him the benefit of the doubt because I felt he needed help. I felt there was something very, very wrong in his life and it seemed that he was quite an unloved child. That's the way that it hit me. I just kind of felt I could help him, but I finally decided I was just knocking my head against a wall and I just had to stop it and I couldn't have him taking my car and keeping it out until 3:00 am or 4:00 am in the morning and telling me, "I'll be back at midnight" and me sitting up waiting.

[Why did he say he was taking the car?]

He told me he was going on trips. He would be gone all these hours and would come back all hepped up. He did this 2 or 3 times. I thought he might be trafficking dope.[17]

In the time he was with Marjorie he became overly dependent on her. He was so afraid of losing her he didn't stand up for himself. Marjorie was Ted's entire life but Ted was only a strong interest to Marjorie at this point. His personality was fragile; it hadn't had the time or the experience to evolve into a mature adult personality. Ted was still a child pretending to be an adult. However, as the 70-year-old nurse indicated, he was far from a normal college student. He was totally unprepared for what would happen next.

Marjorie said of him:

> He was pitifully weak when we argued. This was my main criticism of him after a year and a half of our relationship. He kowtowed to me. He wasn't strong. He wasn't real masculine. If I got mad at him because of something he did he felt apologetic about it. He wouldn't stand up for himself. There was no use getting mad because he didn't react. And, the things I primarily got mad at him for were that he lied when it wasn't necessary that he had to. He would say something he knew would sound good to me rather than telling me the truth.[18]

It was inevitable that the relationship would come to an end. Marjorie was miles ahead of Ted in her social maturity. She came from a wealthy family; her father was a CEO of an international company and he had a dominant executive personality. She admired strength and she wanted a husband with the same ability to make decisions and to take control of his life as she saw in her father. Ted didn't have it.

The Fall

When Marjorie called off the relationship, Ted experienced a very traumatic breakup with a woman with whom he had hoped to share his future. He made an attempt to go on with his life but he was unsuccessful in doing so. It shattered his personality and he was never able to get over it. Ted had no resources to fall back on. He had no coping skills to handle the depression. He had put all of his dreams into Marjorie's hands and he couldn't cope with her strong personality. He couldn't share his pain with his family and he was out of contact with his former friends. His attempt to recover failed. He was likely depressed to the point of considering suicide.

Ted was devastated by the breakup, and he became more anxious and depressed than at any time in the past. He couldn't, as some guys do, go out, get drunk, sleep with a few girls, say,

"To hell with her," and go on with his life. She *was* his life and there was literally no life without her. He felt unattached to everything going on around him. Marjorie was the center of *all* his dreams. He was lost. He was alone. He gave up on Stanford. He gave up his Chinese studies. He would never again talk about working for the federal government. Ted returned to Seattle and attempted to go back to college. He originally chose architecture but the program had no openings so he settled for urban studies. Still, he couldn't get over Marjorie. He couldn't focus in class and he couldn't keep his mind on his studies. There were too many things on campus that reminded him of her.

He had no support system. He couldn't share the depth of his emotions with his parents. He didn't have friends upon whose shoulders he could cry. The loss of his career and his girlfriend were the most severe failures that he had experienced, or ever would experience. He would never recover from it.

His only source of comfort was his pornography, his night stalking, and his detective magazines. The routine fantasy was no longer enough to combat the depth of pain he was feeling. The fantasies had to be stronger, longer, and more detailed.

What had begun as hero fantasies as a child and had turned to romantic love fantasies as a teenager now began to evolve into control and revenge fantasies. In an attempt to extricate himself from powerful lonely and angry emotions he began to sink deeper and deeper into these fantasies. At first in the fantasy it was somebody else engaged in the action and then it became him who was doing it. He dissociated deeply into a scenario and acted out the storyline and, by repeating the same action hundreds of times, began to create an alternate personality within himself. Whenever he desired to do so, he could slip into the frame of this other Entity and watch a revengeful act take place through its eyes. This would happen both when he was alone and when he would see an attractive girl out in public. He later told a girlfriend, Liz, that he would follow girls around campus at night. He said he didn't want to, but he couldn't stop himself from doing so.

Bill stated:

> I never started to think that violence was right until I thought I had a reason for violence. Either revenge or retribution for a perceived wrong. At that point reinforcement started taking place and I would think, "Yeah I would like to do that. Yeah, I would like to do that. Just to pay her back." At that point when I started paying [the girl who hurt me] back [in my thoughts] it started becoming every bit as right to me as a value might be to you, reinforced over time.[19]

Ted wasn't aware that by creating an alternate fantasy personality in his head he was creating neural circuits in his brain which could become permanent mental representatives of this personality.

He dropped out of school and took a trip back to Philadelphia to visit his grandparents. While there he took an excursion to Vermont to see where he was born. Ted also wanted to go to New York to check out the hard-core adult bookstores on 34th Street.

Escalation of an Addiction

Bundy reported to Michaud and Aynesworth:

> There is some kind of weakness that gives rise
> to this individual's interest in the kind of sexual
> activity involving violence that would gradual-
> ly begin to absorb some of his fantasy . . . even-
> tually the interest would become so demand-
> ing toward new material that it could only be
> catered to by what he could find in the dirty
> book stores . . . [20]

The temporary reduction of pain he felt when he was in a
fantasy only whetted his desire for the real thing. He chose to
give in to his pathology rather than to keep it in check. It may

have been during his first trip to Philadelphia when an opportunity presented itself for him to attempt to rape a woman. Bundy describes (always in the third person in these earlier interviews):

> The urge to do something to that [woman he saw] seized him in a way he'd never been affected before. And it seized him strongly. And to the point where, uh, without giving a great deal of thought, he searched around for some instrumentality to uh, uh, attack this woman with . . . there was really no control at this point . . . [21]

She got away which brought an end to the fantasy he was in. Now he was back in full reality.

> What he had done terrified him. Purely terrified him. And he was full of remorse . . . and, you know, he quickly sobered up, as it were . . . The sobering effect of that was to . . . for some time, close up the cracks again. And not do anything. For the first time, he sat back and swore to himself that he wouldn't do something like that again . . . or even, anything that would lead to it . . . within a matter of months, slowly but surely, the impact of this event lost its, uh, deterrent value. And within months he was back, uh, uh, peeping in windows again and slipping back into that old routine.[22]

Return to Politics

When he returned to Seattle, Ted was given an opportunity to work in the Art Fletcher political campaign. This was a very positive experience for him. He soon worked himself into the position of Fletcher's driver, and he attempted to become Fletcher's bodyguard. He was back in his element again, involved in politics, doing dirty tricks during political rallies and whatever else he could do to be at the forefront of an active campaign. He told me that while on a campaign trip he got drunk and a lady put him up for the night. She put him to bed and then climbed in with him. This was possibly the first time he had had sexual intercourse. Regarding his time with Marjorie, he said they would sleep together naked but they didn't have sexual intercourse. When I talked to Marjorie, she confirmed this, saying she wasn't ready for sex. This first sexual experience Ted had was a huge disappointment because he was drunk and he later described the woman as "an hysterical person."

Fletcher lost the election and again Ted was out of a job. Fletcher and other campaign workers praised Bundy for his work but it wasn't enough. His anger and frustration propelled him towards increasingly violent fantasies. At first he didn't want to rape a woman but he wanted to come as close as possible to experiencing it in order to *feel* what it would be like to actually do it.

Three serious consequences of this action stand out. First, he was developing an addiction for sexual revenge. Second, in doing so, he was becoming even more dependent on his private dichotomized life, a social part appearing very normal to everyone who knew him and a second personality that was addicted to violent fantasy. Ted indicated to Michaud and Aynesworth how this personality might develop:

> By peeping in windows, as it were, and watching a woman undress, or watching whatever could be seen, you know, during the evening, and approaching it almost like a project, throwing himself into it, uh, literally for years . . . He gained, you'd say, a terrific amount of . . . at times . . . a great amount of gratification from it and he became increasingly adept at it as anyone becomes adept at anything they do over and over and over again . . . and as the condition develops and its purposes or characteristics become more well defined, it begins to demand more of the attention and time of the individual . . . there is a certain amount of tension, uh, struggle between the normal personality and this, this, uh, psychopathological, uh, entity.[23]

There was undoubtedly a fight between the two parts of him. Still, he couldn't give up either personality. Each was becoming a habituated part of him, likely with its own neural circuits. Ted could shift effortlessly back and forth between them, and his behavior, at this point, was consistent within the realm of each. He would appear normal and likable to his friends and he could shift easily into the violent personality when he was alone.

Once again, as before, Ted had to get away. He had no job, no relationships, and no direction. He told me that he wanted to get a law degree without having to first get his Bachelor's Degree, and he thought he could do it at Temple University in Philadelphia. Was it really that or did he want to go back to the hardcore pornography he found in New York? He was becoming increasingly frustrated with the way his life was going.

Beginning of the Killing Cycle

The first homicide is often not planned. Ted likely had no intent to take the life of a victim but, when the opportunity presented itself, he was unable to stop it from occurring. This created a dramatic and permanent change in his personality and his identity.

Ted was angry and hateful. He viewed others as objects that existed in a world much different from his. They seemed happy and successful. They had families and he didn't. He wanted to have a life like theirs.

Before returning back to Seattle in the early summer of 1969, Ted spent Memorial Day on the New Jersey beach. He met two girls at the beach and struck up a conversation. At that time, he may have entertained a thought of raping them, but I don't believe that he was contemplating killing them. He was from out West, they had never seen him before, and if he raped them and let them go he could escape undetected. However, something went wrong and he killed both of them. These were his first homicides of record.

He had now crossed that final line. He had been holding off from doing this for so long a tremendous amount of stress had built up regarding wanting to hurt but not wanting to kill. At the point of the killing, Ted felt satisfaction. He felt power which frightened him because he had lost control over his destructive impulses.

He had physically destroyed a living person and symbolically destroyed Marjorie, and he felt momentary peace. He had finally gotten his revenge. The killing cycle was complete, the process permanently fixed in place, and the only thing that would stop him from killing again would be if he were caught and locked up or killed himself. The intense high and the feeling of peace justified the action. Now the dark side was extremely strong, but Ted's negative image of himself was also very strong.

He was fearful of getting caught so he likely checked the crime scene to ascertain the possibility of having left evidence.

Rescued by Liz

Following a first homicide, a killer may attempt to live a normal life. He is fearful of getting caught and he is fearful that he could do it again. Ted found a person who could love him and support him in his education and career. It was too little, too late.

Ted returned to the West Coast, got a job, and met a woman who remained a loyal supporter until after he was convicted of attempting to kidnap Carol DaRonch.

Liz Kendall met Ted in the Sandpiper Tavern on October 31, 1969. They both got drunk and Ted spent the night at her apartment. She was impressed by his looks, his clothes, and that he didn't attempt to make love to her that night. She quickly fell in love with Ted and Ted with her. She saw Ted as a future husband to replace her failed marriage, and stepfather to her daughter; and Ted saw Liz as an anchoring force to bring him back to some degree of normalcy. At first he was happy with the relationship, as was she with him. Ted treated her daughter as a beloved stepdaughter. He spent time with Liz's family in Utah and demonstrated genuine interest in them. It was working so well that Liz began to pressure Ted to get married.

In *The Phantom Prince: My Life with Ted Bundy,* Liz wrote:

> I was amazed and pleased at how much Ted liked our domestic scene. He seemed hungry for family life. He took [my daughter] Tina and me out to all of his favorite places; the public market; the main street of the University District called "the Ave," where we browsed through used book and record stores; the International District, where we had Chinese food and Ted tried out his limited Chinese on the patient waiters. We made love every chance we got. I had never felt this close to any man before.[24]

Deterioration of the Relationship with Liz

Once a person has developed an appetite for killing it is very difficult to give it up.

Ted did try to be a good companion to Liz and provide a positive stepfather image to her daughter. However, by now, Ted was a full-fledged psychopath. He had luxury items in his apartment, all stolen. He pacified Liz by telling her that he loved her and was willing to marry her, and he went so far as to get a marriage license. However, his relationship was built on lies. He was extremely dependent on her, partly for the bit of stability she offered him at that point in his life and partly because she was willing to take care of him. Fortunately for Ted, Liz was deeply in love with him and she wasn't ready to give him up. When the relationship was good, it was very good. Ted had a personality that people could admire. Years later, a highly respected woman in Salt Lake expressed to me how impressed she was with him when he visited her family. She said that she would have been happy to have her daughter go out with him and even to marry him.

Graduation from College

When Ted graduated from the University of Washington in June of 1972 he was 25 years old. He majored in psychology and graduated with honors. Liz gave him a yellow six-man rubber raft for a graduation gift. This raft would play an important role in his life in the future.

One of his professors wrote:

> Mr. Bundy is undoubtedly one of the top undergraduate students in our department. Indeed, I would place him in the top 1% of undergraduate students with whom I have interacted both here at the University of Washington and at Purdue University. He is exceedingly bright, personable, highly motivated and

conscientious. He conducts himself more like a
young professional than like a student.[25]

Very impressive.

During this same period of time just prior to his graduation
he was part of a work-study program run by the Seattle Crisis
Clinic taking crisis phone calls twice a week. It was here that he
met and worked with Ann Rule, a writer of true crime. Rule
was very impressed by him when she worked alongside him.
Her opinion eventually changed. In *The Stranger Beside Me*, Ann
Rule expressed her feelings about Ted. She wrote:

> I don't know that I—or anyone else who ever
> knew Ted or studied him—has the key to who
> he really was. I doubt that even *he* knew that. I
> do know that my own view of him has evolved
> in a way exactly opposite of the public's accep-
> tance of Ted as a cold character. When I read
> my own evaluation of him in the '70s, I realize
> I had a long way to go to achieve true accuracy.
> In the almost three decades since I laid eyes
> on Ted, I have been forced to accept increas-
> ingly grisly truth. The human mind—my own
> included—creates elaborate unconscious path-
> ways to let it deal with horror.
>
> My memory of Ted Bundy is clear but
> bifurcated; I remember *two* Teds. One is the
> young man who sat beside me two nights
> a week in Seattle's Crisis Clinic. The other is
> the voyeur, the rapist, the killer and the necro-
> philiac. Try as I might, I still can't bring the
> two images together. Looking at them under an

> imaginary microscope, I cannot superimpose
> the murderer over the promising student. And
> I am not alone. Most of the people who knew
> him struggle with the same dichotomy. And so
> I deal, always, with separate Teds.[26]

Both his psychology professor and Ann Rule were very impressed with the Ted Bundy they rubbed shoulders with week after week. Was the caring, sensitive Bundy that Rule worked with on the crisis line simply a psychopathic façade? Was it completely fake? I don't think so. I think the "good" side of him was who he *wanted* to be. It was the side of him who could be intelligent, sensitive, friendly, and a team player. He could function normally for brief periods of time. However, when the dark side of him—the part he called the Entity—was triggered, he couldn't be at peace until he satisfied its urges.

Ted also needed to find a job. He had a degree in psychology and he had been working on a crisis line, so he had some impressive credentials which got him hired on at Seattle's Harborview Hospital to work with psychiatric outpatients. This was an opportunity for him to gain some control of himself. However, he had indulged in his pathologically lifestyle for too long, and from this point on he would gradually lose control at a fairly rapid rate. This downhill spiral would continue unstopped until he was arrested by Sergeant Hayward in Utah.

Ted was still with Liz and still promised her that they would be getting married. However, he was reaching out for other relationships. Ted needed Liz but she wasn't enough for him. He was still in touch with Marjorie from time to time but only through friendly phone calls.

He spent the Fourth of July with another woman and Liz became enraged. Ted cried and professed his undying love for

Liz, and he called off the relationship with this other woman. From Liz's point of view, once again things seemed fine between the two of them.

However, things really weren't fine. Ted was sinking even more deeply into pornography and his fantasy life. Every disaster in his life pulled him deeper into the abyss that he had created for himself. He still continued to steal. His thoughts and fantasies became obsessions he couldn't control. His dark side was extremely powerful and normal relationships didn't satisfy him. Traditional sexual encounters were not exciting enough. He was spending more and more of his time in his fantasy world, and the demarcation between the two worlds in which he lived in was extremely thin.

One woman reported to me:

> Ted was spaced out on several occasions. One night he was walking to his home and Liz and I passed him on the sidewalk. He didn't even recognize Liz, who at the time was his girl-friend. I have seen him spaced out many times. His response to anxiety was to space out.[27]
>
> I often thought he was ignoring me. He told me he felt inferior to me and he wondered why I would ever go with him. He seemed to have no friends and he never spoke of any.[28]

She worked with him at the Center and added:

> People at Harborview Mental Health Center were very critical of him because he came and went as he chose. In therapy he was harsh and cold and people were dismayed. He

showed anger toward women and others. He lacked understanding of the clients. He showed confidence outwardly but had strong inferior feelings underneath. He made a point of talking against his family and the fact that Bundy wasn't his true father. Others saw him as weird and an intellectual phony. People were generally unimpressed with him.[29]

It's clear that by the summer of 1972 Ted's pathology was beyond his ability to understand it, let alone control it. He had his Bachelor's degree, he had a job, he had Liz who was completely devoted to him, and he had other women who were willing to have relationships with him. Still, it wasn't enough. He was seeking something but he couldn't find it.

The Governor Dan Evans Campaign

In the lives of many serial killers, events occur that seem to offer the killer what he has been seeking. Logically, one could say that he doesn't need to go on killing because he has found stability through success in relationships and employment. However, a process of destruction has become firmly implanted in his brain and it can't be permanently eradicated.

Once more Ted would have the opportunity to bring stability to his life. He worked in Governor Dan Evans' reelection campaign of 1972 and served as assistant to Ross Davis, chairman of the Washington State Republican Party, in 1973. He had been accepted into the University of Utah Law School to begin his studies in the fall of 1973. He notified them that he had been in an accident (which was a lie) and would be unable to attend.

Through a recommendation from a friend, he applied and was accepted into the law program at the University of Puget Sound to start in the fall of 1973, which once more put him back on track for a law degree. Meanwhile, he was employed and was obtaining recognition for his campaign work.

A campaign coworker said of him:

> He was a champion of causes. He was concerned about the situation of the Blacks, of all minorities. He was unhappy with the injustices of society and he wanted to do something about them.[30]

Governor Dan Evans was reelected for another term. Ted was ecstatic since he had worked hard in the campaign and had had personal contact with Evans. The celebration was in January, 1973. Ted and Liz went to buy her an outfit for the ball and in the process Ted caught a purse snatcher. Liz felt out of place at the ball and slipped away from the crowd and got drunk.

Ted briefly got a job studying white collar crime with the Seattle Crime Commission which was followed by an even better job working for the King County Budget Office. In the spring of 1973 he was appointed Assistant Chairman of the Washington State Republican Central Committee, a job he enjoyed. Things were going quite well for him.

However, during the early summer of 1973, Liz was growing weary of Ted's lack of commitment to their relationship. Liz accepted an invitation to help a man sail his catamaran followed by a bicycle trip in Victoria, British Columbia. Ted was extremely irate and depressed, and he wrote her a series of love letters, again telling Liz how much he loved her and needed her. Ted was distraught by Liz's lack of loyalty to him, despite his own unfaithfulness. He was extremely insecure and the thought of being alone terrified him. She called off the relationship with this other man and once more things seemed to be all right with Ted.

When I conducted my assessment of him for the court in April of 1976, Ted talked about this incident. It was one of only two or three times that I could see a definite change in his eyes and his facial expression. He said, "I felt terribly hurt. I went home and sulked. My world was destroyed. That was the last straw." He was quiet for a few moments, regained his composure, and then said that he and Liz made up and both cried. However, this widened a deep crack in his personality. It may have been around this time that he killed his next victim.

Reuniting with Marjorie

When a person is deeply in love and, against his wishes, their lover breaks it off, there is often a desire to rekindle the relationship with the hope that this time it will work out.

In the fall of 1973, Ted began attending graduate-level night classes at University of Puget Sound (UPS) and, at first, he made progress. He occasionally took Liz to some of his classes, and he was leading her to believe they would get married later, when he completed law school. Even though he and his first love, Marjorie, had ended their romantic relationship in the summer of 1967, they had continued to be in periodic contact with each other since then. Undoubtedly, he kept her informed of his successes with the intent to impress her of the changes in his personality. He visited her in San Francisco and spent a week attempting to show her how different he was. She was cautious at first but after a couple of days he succeeded and she invited him to stay in her apartment. She told me that she saw a 180 degree change in him. He wasn't the shy kid she knew six years earlier. He appeared to be in charge of his life; he had graduated from college and was working for the government, and he had been accepted into law school.

Perhaps he showed her the glowing recommendation from his college professor. He may have wowed her with his political activities. Whatever he did, he did it well and he was able to convince Marjorie that it would be worthwhile for them to reconsider a future with each other. They made plans to get together in September, 1973 and to actively explore the possibility of getting married then. All the time he was doing this, Liz believed that Ted loved only her and that marriage was in their future.

What was Ted after? It wasn't Liz because she didn't have the personality he was looking for in a politician's wife. She had strong dependency issues and a serious alcohol problem. He had a clear picture of what she was like from the Governor Dan Evans victory party. While he wasn't ready to give her up, he believed that it could never work out with her.

He had never fully stopped loving Marjorie. Did he seriously believe that Marjorie was the one, the politician's wife, the power behind future success for him, or was he simply out to get even with her for dropping him? Six years earlier he had been deeply in love with her and perhaps thought that if he could rekindle that love, this time it might work out. Liz was a convenience, a necessity until something better came along. Marjorie was hope for a future. A politician's wife. A rekindling of a dream that he had had when he first dated her.

Ted had held a number of positions with the state government but was unsatisfied with one thing or another with almost all of them. Life for him was not at all what he thought it should be. It's possible that his move to reestablish a relationship with Marjorie was an act of desperation, an attempt to pick up where they had left off. An attempt to begin again, to return to who he was when they were in love, when their relationship was young and exciting. That had been the happiest time of his life; all of his memories since then were stormy and violent. One never fully gets over their first deep love. Perhaps he thought that if he were successful this time it would erase, to some degree, the pathology that had accrued since they had broken up.

Christmas 1973

A time may come in a serial killer's life when he makes one last desperate attempt to extricate himself from the inevitable destruction that he feels lies before him.

Marjorie flew up to Seattle in September 1973 and they re-affirmed their love for each other and spoke of the possibility of getting married. They made plans to get together during the Christmas holidays to talk seriously about their future.

However, there was a distinct difference now. He had taken the lives of innocent victims on at least two occasions and he had an obsessive drive to kill again. During the fall of 1973, Ted would go out into the night and watch college girls through their windows . . . and pretend. There were times that he would pick up young girls who were hitchhiking and he would not harm them. On these occasions he felt relief that he was able to resist the urge to kill, which he didn't want to do because it would ruin any chance he had for a career. However, he was almost beyond the point of being able to control his impulses.

Liz spent Christmas with her parents in Utah. Marjorie flew up to Seattle to spend Christmas with Ted. Ted and Marjorie skied, made love, and talked of marriage. Ted proposed marriage to Marjorie on New Year's Eve and she accepted. The plan was for her to fly back to San Francisco, tell her family and friends, and begin planning the wedding which would take place that spring. She left on New Year's Day.

Whether or not he had any plans to actually marry her is an open question. Ted told me that he initially felt that she would be the ideal wife for the type of career he was seeking, but he also said he didn't love her. He said that Marjorie would "fly into fits of rage" at some of the things he did such as locking his keys in the car or forgetting to pick up some tomatoes. He felt that Marjorie was more impatient and high strung than Liz. Why then did he propose marriage? Ted told me, "I feel it was to demonstrate that I could have married her." His victory, however, was empty and it brought him no satisfaction.

Ted said that after she got on the plane he couldn't get in the car fast enough to get back to Liz, who had just returned from her holiday in Utah.

He said it was like a "breath of fresh air" when he saw Liz He exchanged gifts with her and talked about their holidays. Ted lied about the expensive gifts that Liz saw in his apartment. He told her his mother had given them to him. Liz felt that something was not quite right because she knew his mother couldn't afford those gifts. However, she didn't say anything about her suspicions.

Was winning Marjorie over only a ruse to get revenge? I don't think so. Ted didn't gloat over his triumph. He didn't return to Liz with a deep sense of satisfaction that he had finally gotten even with Marjorie for all the pain she had caused him. He didn't go back to Liz with a belief that he could now get on with his life. I believe that he was hoping that it *would* work out with Marjorie. He wasn't happy with Liz, he hadn't found satisfaction with other girls he had briefly dated, and now he wasn't satisfied with Marjorie.

The Killing Begins – January 1974

When the last-ditch attempt to hold it together doesn't work, a killer may more fully give in to his pathology. If he can't prevent it, he harvests it. He stops fighting the urges and focuses instead on stealth and prevention of detection. He and his pathology are now one and the same. He may feel like God because he can give and take away life.

Bill, the killer quoted previously, talked about the constant urge to strike out at some victim:

> When you start believing you are at the top of the hill, that you're top dog, it becomes danger-ous because you become God. No law applies to you. You make the rules. One doesn't have a

conscious sense of feeling like God, but I think that what . . . is true is that you start acting like God in that you feel that everything around you is yours to do with as you please.

It's not so much a sense of ownership as entitlement. You are entitled. You have the right to do whatever you want to do, to snatch up whomever you want to snatch up, to hurt whosoever's feelings you want to hurt, to take from anyone you want to take from, without censor. Intellectually you know that's not the case. Inside, you have this semi-conscious awareness that's not really true. But the *feeling* is what overwhelms that. Passion completely obliterates reason.

You act on the basis that you have the right to do whatever you want to do. One thing I would like to say is that those feelings are always there, but it really isn't acted upon until that compulsion strikes, that altering. That almost split personality type of thing. It's not a true multiple personality. But when you experience the psychological fall and you get into that cycle, everything changes. It's a metamorphosis.[31]

Ted had now lost all hope of ever finding what he was looking for. His personality was so fractured that he could no longer exert any control over his obsessive need to kill. He was completely alone without the emotionally satisfying support that he needed. Not Marjorie. Not Liz. Not his family. Not his career. Even though he had a number of possibilities, he felt completely alone.

He was a passive observer to a force far superior to any strength he could muster against it. The force within him was triggered when he was aroused, angry, depressed, or when something he saw or thought about thrust it into his mind. It wasn't there all the time but it was becoming more frequent. From this point on, until he was arrested in Utah on August 15, 1975, Ted would not be able to stop seeking out and killing victims. It was not that he didn't want to stop, it was that he couldn't. He had been giving life to this Entity within him for so many years, turning it into a person, allowing it to be in control when it suited him. It was almost as if he had created a split personality.

Ted's killing spree began with an attack on a coed in the Seattle University District on January 4, 1974, just three days after asking Marjorie to marry him. He sat outside this girl's apartment until 2:00 am while she was upstairs watching TV. He had undoubtedly watched her before so he knew the intricacies of how to get into her apartment without risking being detected. When she came downstairs for bed, he waited until she was asleep and then quietly entered and viciously attacked her in her bed and left her for dead. The level of skill in the attack was not that of a first-time offender. Ted had planned every detail of the attack, suggesting that he had been anticipating this possibility for some time.

There was now an even greater change in his personality and identity. He had no power over this other side of him. He couldn't stop so he indulged in it.

On February 1, 1974, Bundy broke into University of Washington (UW) coed Lynda Ann Healy's room and knocked her unconscious, dressed her in her jeans and a shirt, wrapped her in a bed sheet, and carried her away. He had now killed at least three girls while continuing to hold down a job, go to law school, tell Liz that he was still in love with her, and have Marjorie plan a rather elaborate wedding in San Francisco. Dressing her in jeans and a shirt and carrying Lynda Ann Healy off suggests the depth of his pathological fantasies.

On March 12, 1974, Ted kidnapped and murdered Donna Gail Manson in Olympia, Washington; then Susan Rancourt from the campus of Central Washington State College; Kathy Parks from Oregon State University in Corvallis; and Brenda Ball from Burien, Washington. The list goes on and on. He couldn't stop, and after he began his killing spree in January, it didn't seem that he wanted to. He seemed completely given to the killing and so spent much of his energy on avoiding detection. He deposited some bodies of his victims in the same location on Taylor Mountain where he knew the animals would scatter the bones. He committed the crimes in different police jurisdictions because he had learned from his research on rape victims that the police from different jurisdictions didn't share information with each other.

Ted couldn't concentrate on his studies and he likely wanted to leave the area before he got caught. He reapplied to the University of Utah Law School and was again accepted.

Ted and Liz weren't getting along very well. One night in March, Liz came home to find that Ted had persuaded the landlord to let him in to her apartment. He was in tears and said he was failing school because he couldn't concentrate on his studies. He said he didn't know what was wrong. They decided that UPS may not be the right school for him. He dropped out of school without taking the final exams. In June, Ted got a job with the State Department of Emergency Services in Olympia, Washington, a two hour drive from Seattle, so Ted and Liz saw less of each other.

An Attempt to Change?

At times a serial killer will make an attempt to stop killing.

Ted was a Baptist when he was a child but he became an atheist. It was therefore somewhat surprising that he became involved with the Mormon Church during the summer of 1975. This was a dramatic departure from his religious beliefs, or lack of them. He took the missionary lessons and was baptized into the Mormon Church. I was very curious about his reasoning because he didn't believe in an organized religion, didn't believe in God, was breaking all of the standards of the Church, and lied to the missionaries and the bishop who interviewed him for baptism. When I asked him about this, he said, "I was tired of my own failure to find direction and stability in my life. I wanted to adopt a more disciplined approach. I felt my lifestyle could be improved. I felt there was warmth of fraternity with the church."

I asked him what was lacking in his life. He said, "Oh, maybe like when one sees a painting and you want it because it represents something you want to be a part of." He said he felt that by being a member of the church he could get the strength to stop smoking and drinking. His LDS bishop and the missionaries who converted him described him as seemingly honest and sincere.

Why did he join the Church? I believe that at least part of the reason was because he wanted to stop killing. He had a chance to finally get his law degree, which could open up a career in politics he had yearned for since he was a child. It's a stretch of imagination to believe that he was completely unaware he was taking more risks and that it was only a matter of time before he was caught. The other time he would show a consistent interest in religion was in the months leading up to his execution.

It was soon after this that he was apprehended by Sergeant Bob Hayward of the Utah Highway Patrol at 2:30 am on the morning of August 16, 1975. He was arrested because he had what appeared to be burglary tools in his car. He told Sergeant Hayward that he had been watching a movie at the local outdoor drive-in but he misidentified the name of the film that was playing that night. He was booked and released on bail.

Meanwhile, the authorities in Seattle were sending word to Salt Lake that they had a Ted Bundy who could be the "Ted" they were looking for. Also, the Carol DaRonch case came up because her abductor had tried to kidnap her with handcuffs and Bundy had handcuffs in his car when Sgt. Hayward apprehended him. Some of the authorities in Salt Lake didn't want to pursue an investigation of Bundy because he looked too clean. However, Detective Jerry Thompson insisted on pursuing it.

Detective Jerry Thompson's Investigation

I interviewed Detective Jerry Thompson of the Salt Lake to get his opinion about Ted.

> Al Carlisle: What was Ted like when you first began investigating him?
>
> Jerry Thompson: He is the exception to anything I've worked on, let's put it that way. He's the exception to the rule. He was very nice. He was very polite. He was educated. He thought things out. He thought he was better than everybody else and I think that was his downfall.
>
> A.C: What did you see in him when you were doing the investigation?

J.T: Well, I guess just his action, the way he talked. You got the impression that [he thought] he knew more than you. I guess the thing that disturbed me was the very first night that I met him when I brought him up from the jail. I had never seen him. I didn't know anything about him. Took him to his apartment. I had never had a guy apologize to me— and haven't yet—for him making me work so hard. Not apologizing for his actions at all because he [said he was] totally innocent. He [believed he was] a victim of his circumstances. He was very, very neat like I say. Liked to talk and that was part of his downfall too. He talked too much. He was an individual you had to watch. We took him into his front room. I had another deputy with me. He sat down on the couch and I started looking around. He offered me the world. I didn't like that at all.

A.C: How do you mean?

J.T: Oh, whatever you want, sure. Can I help you here? Do you want to go through here? Just do this. That's not just a con because they don't act like that. That's not John Q Citizen who is innocent because they are very upset that you're tearing their house apart. That disturbed me. I would watch him when he wasn't looking at me. I remember I was on my hands and knees looking in his bedroom and I'd kind of look over to the side at him like this [demonstrates]. He watched me like a hawk. I could see his eyes and the minute I'd turn towards him he would turn his head away. He was studying me. He was watching me very close. I could observe that he was getting nervous. I'm sure he was wondering: What's he looking for? What's he going to find? From that night on, I said, there's something radically wrong here. This is a different personality than I have dealt with in my life and I really don't like it.

A.C: In what other ways did you see him as being different?

J.T: Well, you know, the guy was pleasant. He called me. How do you get a guy to call you? A hundred times! This guy calls you on the phone! He totally calls you on the phone! I can still hear that sneering laugh of his to-day. I'd like to strangle him. Laugh and, "Hi Jerry. How're you doing?" You know, like he's my friend.

A.C: What would he talk about?

JT: Oh whatever. If he'd think you might have found out something, "I know you're busy on me. I really hate to bother you. After all, you get paid for it. It's a job and stuff. I don't know why you're working so hard on me because I'm not the guy you think I am." And I'd ask him, "Who do you think I think you are?" "Well," he'd say, "you tell me," and he'd laugh. And I said, "No, I'm waiting for you to tell me." As it went on, later on, he turned around and said,

"You think I'm the individual involved in these killings and stuff." But then he'd ask me, "Why are you following me, Jerry?" I'd say, "I'm not following you." "Oh yes you were. I saw you at the University up there." "Yeah, I saw you up at the University too but I wasn't following you. I'm doing my job. Yeah, I'm working on you but I wasn't following you."

A.C: Did he seem to be calling you to find out what you knew?

J.T: Oh, sure! He's trying to find out what I knew. Yeah. And he'd say, "Yeah you are Jerry. Your car was parked around in back. Most guys park out in front unless you're hiding." I said, "Did that bother you why I was parked around there?" He said, "Well, no." I said, "I'll give you a big secret if it will make you feel better, Ted." I said, "The parking lot is full. It's hard to get a parking spot." I said, "You go around in back where the faculty parks and you can drive right up and walk in." I said, "I'm a lazy individual." But I said, "If that bugs you, no I'm not following you but I saw you up there sneaking from door to door." When we had surveillance on him, I knew that he was watching us. He'd wave. I believe it built his ego. I'm smarter than them dumb cops, you know. Even when he washed his car and tore it apart, everything in it, we took photos. He knew that. It built his ego.

A.C: He called me from Colorado after he escaped and got caught.

J.T: Oh yeah, he called me so much from Colorado I wanted to strangle him.

A.C: Why did he keep calling you?

J.T: He kept calling on his murder case over there before it went to court. "Well you know, I'm my own attorney and I need this or I need that, I need this report." I'd just laugh at him. He said, "You know, I have a right to this," and I said, "You know Ted, you don't have a right to nothing as far as I'm concerned." "Well, you're not listening to me." I said, "No, I hear you well." I said, "I'll give you anything you want. Just tell me one thing. Where's Debbie [Kent]?" He'd sigh and he'd laugh, "Who is Debbie?" I said, "You play your silly games. I'll play mine." We'd do that time and time again. He'd say, "I can't do that Jerry." "What do you mean you can't do that?" He'd say, "I'm not going to help you. I'm not going to make you look good. I'm not going to make you look like a hero." I said, "I ain't a hero. I ain't nothing." I said, "I don't care if you tell me or who you tell. There's a million ways [to tell someone where her body is]. Just let her be found." I'd try to play on him. I said, "You know, I don't know if you've got any feelings inside you or not. You claim you do. If you do, if you've got a daughter, wouldn't you want to know where she was at?" I said, "Show me if you've got anything inside you." I said, "But don't tell me. Don't incriminate yourself. I could care less [how you do it]. There's a million ways." "Oh no," he said, "You've got so many ways of finding out things." He'd go on talking and you knew right then that he's telling you everything but that he did it. "You know, I can't do that," he'd say. If he'd go any further than that he'd catch himself or he'd know that you'd caught him on that and he'd back right off.

I was criticized when I first started working on him. "How can you get involved? This kid's a graduate from college. He's going to law school. He's a sharp dresser. He's been involved with campaigns." I said, "The guy's a total phony." [The way he acted] totally disturbed my mind.

A.C: Because of his apartment?

J.T: Oh yeah. The way he was. The way he talked. I don't know if you'll ever find another like that.

A.C: What was his apartment like?

J.T: Immaculate. He even had his shoes lined up.

A.C: Clothes lined up?

J.T: Yep. Everything. In fact, I asked him, "Have you ever been in the military?" He said, "No, why do you ask?" "The only place I have ever seen in my life, hangers, in the military they are two fingers apart." His closet was like that. I said, "I have never seen that before in my life. You must have been in the military." "Oh no, that's just the way I hang them up."

A.C: Did you see any deterioration in him as the investigation continued?

J.T: He got more nervous. Totally more nervous. I don't know how to describe it. His eyes told the story. Rather than being the happy-go-lucky individual, more and more that look changed. His look, I don't know if it was fear or if it was hate in his eyes. That became more and more as things wore on. He loved attention too. He *loved* attention. He wanted everybody in the world to think that he was the neatest thing in the world.

A.C: How did he react when you finally arrested him for attempted kidnapping?

J.T: I think he was overwhelmed and yet I think he had a sigh of relief because the arrest was not for murder. I think he was really looking for Murder One and when we charged him with the kidnapping, at first he was as white as a ghost. He was trembling and rather than me telling him I handed him the paper. He read it and said, "Oh God, is that all?" I said, "You were waiting for the Murder One weren't you Ted?" I said, "That's next." Like I said, he was really uptight.[32]

Trial, Conviction, Evaluation, Escape

When Ted was arrested for the attempted abduction of Carol DaRonch, the news of his arrest broke in Seattle. There was shock and disbelief among those who had known him and had worked with him in political campaigns. Ted Bundy was described to me in glowing terms as an up-and-coming politician. People I talked to said he was intelligent, organized, very ambitious, and that he worked well with those in political campaigns who were in authority over him as well as those who worked alongside him. He was a team leader. Surely a mistake had been made, they said. The cops in Salt Lake must not know what they're doing. It couldn't be *our* Ted, not the Ted we have worked with so closely and intensely in these campaigns. Family and friends immediately began a fund for his defense.

It's not that the people in the Northwest were simply standing up for one of their own. Ted was all of these things they mentioned. It testifies to the fact that Bundy had two very strong personality styles, and when he was impressive, he was very impressive.

Ted and his lawyer, John O'Connell, one of the best defense lawyers in practice, decided that a trial by judge would be advantageous to Ted's chances of acquittal. Judge Stewart Hanson Jr. was known to be a fair judge. However, after a week in trial, Judge Hanson felt there was enough evidence to find Ted guilty. Before sentencing Ted to prison, he was sent to the Utah State Prison for a 90-Day Evaluation.

On June 30, 1976, the day of sentencing, the evaluations had been completed and were sent to the court. Judge Hansen allowed Ted to respond to the psychological and psychiatric reports. With anger and tears in his eyes he vociferously refuted the conclusions of the reports, particularly mine. He went over my report point by point saying that each of my statements would apply to hundreds of others, and he concluded, "This (holding up my report) was written to conform to the verdict." He added, "I suggest you ask yourself, what's been accomplished? Was the sacrifice of my life worth it all? An eye for an eye, measure for measure, is child's play in comparison to what you are about to do today. Yes, I will be a candidate for treatment! Not for anything I have done but for what the system has done to me!"

As I sat and listened to his rebuttal of my report and I saw his tear-filled eyes and heard the bitter hostility in his voice, I wondered if I had judged him too harshly. If O'Connell had put me on the stand and drilled me on each of the points I made, I couldn't have declared that these impressions applied only to Ted Bundy and not to hundreds of others. What then were my conclusions from the twenty or more hours I spent with Ted and from the psychological tests I gave him? First, there were the many positive things that people said about him. The following are some of the negative conclusions I found:

1. He was a private person and wouldn't reveal himself to others. He didn't want to be known by others.
2. He became defensive and evasive when any of his girlfriends tried to get information from him.
3. Outwardly, he looked very adequate. This masked strong feelings of inadequacy underneath.
4. He couldn't handle ambiguity.
5. Lack of a biological father was very significant to him.
6. He viewed women as more competent than men.
7. He demonstrated a strong dependency on women for emotional support and yet he couldn't settle down with one. He said he resented dependency and yet he seemed to most resent his own dependency.
8. He would get very upset when people would say negative things about him.
9. There were a number of people coming in and out of his life. Most relationships were brief, suggesting instability. He would hurt deeply when he would lose someone. There was a strong sense of futility about him.
10. He was reluctant to accept help or support from anyone (except for financial support). He wanted relationships with people on his terms and he wanted to be in control of the relationships at all times. He was egocentric. It was extremely important for him to be in control of his emotions, of interpersonal relationships, and interviews. He had a very strong fear of being hurt and he put up strong defenses against getting close, including being touched. He had an obsession regarding controlling and structuring, and he ran from a situation or relationship when it didn't work.
11. He showed strong suspicions regarding people playing games or trying to trick him, and he was always on guard. He was a very perceptive person.

12. There was a strong theme of having been put down, humiliated, and made fun of.

13. He felt a strong sense of loneliness.

14. He exhibited rapid changes in moods from pleasant to angry to depressed.

15. He lacked outward indications of guilt and tried to conceal his anxiety. However, he showed it through deep sighs and heavy perspiration.

16. His behavior was not modifiable by fear. He claimed, "I don't have fears. Fear, pain, and punishment don't stick with me."

Ted was sentenced for a term of one to fifteen years at the Utah State Prison. Had he stayed out of trouble he would have served a few years and then he would have been free again. However, while he was housed at the Medium Facility, he began to make plans for an escape. An officer caught on to what he was doing—constructing a fake wristband ID—and he was transferred to the Maximum Facility. I continued visiting with him, and I found him to be friendly and he seemed to enjoy our conversations. I was surprised at this, having seen the bitterness he demonstrated towards me in court. He could easily have refused to see me in prison and there would have been no repercussions. He treated me as if I were his friend and he talked freely with me.

Ted got along with the other inmates, partly because his status as a killer put him at the top of the convict hierarchy and partly because he was working on his own legal briefs and he was willing to help other inmates with theirs. Some inmates reported that he would space out at times and seemed to be unaware of what was going on around him. A couple of inmates said Ted would carry on an argument with himself in his cell. After a short stay in prison in Utah, Ted was transferred to Colorado for ongoing investigations of two homicides in that state.

Ted was in his element in Colorado. He was acting as his own lawyer with the help and advice of top defense lawyers. He had access to law books and he had his own credit card and his own phone in his cell. People throughout the West were aware of Ted Bundy which made him famous in his own eyes.

Ted was a lonely and insecure person. He needed constant attention. He craved being needed and admired. Now, finally, he was getting it. He believed that he could demonstrate to the police and the prosecutors that he was more skilled in the law than they were. Ted wouldn't have to go to law school to demonstrate his legal acumen; he could show it in court and it would be reported in the news media throughout Colorado, Utah, and Washington, and probably in many other places around the world. Even though he knew he was guilty of killing many women, Ted was able to portray himself as innocent.

While he was working on his legal briefs for court, however, he was also planning for an opportunity to escape. The opportunity did present itself, and on June 6, 1977, when everyone briefly stepped out of the courtroom and left Bundy alone, he dropped out of the open second-story window and headed up into the hills. It wasn't an impulsive decision; he had been practicing jumping from the top bed in his cell to the floor, strengthening his legs, and he had worn heavy clothing on that day even though it was warm. Ted was an exceptionally keen observer, always aware of himself in connection with everything and everyone around him. He felt he had a sixth sense about these things. He had stood by the open window on other court occasions, and he had an exceptionally good ability to convince people he was dealing with that he was perfectly cooperative. It was as though what people saw outwardly in him was so definite that it allowed the full truth to remain invisible. Only his victims saw the real Ted Bundy.

After he slipped out of the window, he headed for the hills. Shortly after he escaped, he called me saying he wanted my impressions of his escape. I have always felt that this was evidence of his loneliness, his need for people, his insecurity, and his need for recognition and acceptance by authority figures. He never did call me Dr. Carlisle. It was always Al, and he also referred to others by their first name.

He was caught a few days later because he had exhausted himself and had misjudged what it would take to get over the mountains.

He was moved to a new jail, still with his own phone and credit card. He called me from his jail cell:

> Ted Bundy: How are you doing?
>
> Al Carlisle: I'm doing all right, Ted. How are you doing?
>
> T.B: Well, I'm hanging in there. I just got the bug last week and just wanted to chat with you briefly.
>
> A.C: How are things going for you over there?
>
> T.B: Well, quite well frankly. I was just talking to someone the other day and the experience of coming over here is one of those, you know, good things, bad things experiences. If I hadn't come over here I probably wouldn't be looking at a new trial in the Carol DaRonch case and a number of things have opened up and I sup-

pose that if I had to spend several years behind bars, I might as well spend a little here, a little there (laughs).

A.C: Are they treating you pretty good?

T.B: Yah, sure they are. They've developed this paranoia about me. They have this unrealistic fear that I'm going to escape or something.

A.C: I can't imagine where they're getting that from (laughs).

T.B: Yah, exactly (laughs). Al, I just wanted to call you up, mainly . . . there's a lot of things that's been happening. My escape venture which has caused a great furor of activity around here and I guess some complicity over there and now we're looking at what looks like a 95% chance of a new trial in the Carol DaRonch case and this case over here gets curiouser and curiouser because they've added a couple of Utah transactions, alleged transactions, in an attempt to gain a conviction in the Colorado case. I don't know . . . I've been so overwhelmed by work recently . . . that ah . . . you know, there's just a lot to do. You know, way back when, I guess it was back in April when I decided to represent myself in this case I could hear Al Carlisle saying, "Yah, I knew you'd try something like that" (laughs).

A.C: Yah, I assumed you would (laughs).

T.B: I remember one time you commented . . . I think it was something I read in your report . . . that I like to do things myself and I have a hard time entrusting things to others.

A.C: Uh huh.

T.B: I was wondering if you've had any impression about all that you've been hearing about me . . . and . . .

A.C: How do you mean?

T.B: Well, the escape and everything. I wonder what your impression of that was, from a party who knows me but didn't have an opportunity to speak to me after that happened.

A.C: I had mixed impressions. I was wondering if you were really getting uptight and the pressure looked like it was on. I was wondering if it looked like, in your mind, like you were going to be convicted so when the opportunity was there, you just took it. In your own mind, what was happening?

T.B: You know, I'd given it a great deal of thought. I'd been in the Pitkin County Jail, which is in Aspen, from January 31st until April the 11th which is 73 days. I have all this memorized. In Aspen it was an open affair. It's seven cells and all the doors are open all the time. The place had been built in 1887. Here was where I could come out and talk to other prisoners, going in their cell. And then they moved me down here—this is part of the escape because I was a security risk. They put me in a six by twelve by eight foot high cell and ordered no one to speak to me. Quite frankly, that's why I decided to represent myself. This [tension] was building up and building up and over the months I'd noticed a number of opportunities to just walk right out of the courthouse, but I didn't know how to put it all together. I was very concerned about what people would think.

People said, weren't you afraid that someone would shoot you or something? No, it was one of the lower fears in my hierarchy of fears. But, I don't know, that day I came there and I thought a great deal about escape and I didn't know if I had the guts to do it quite frankly. The guard went outside for a smoke and there was not one person in the whole courtroom. The windows were open and the fresh air was blowing through and the sky was blue and I said, I'm ready to go, and I walked to the window and I jumped out (laughs). And I started chugging.

I had no plan. I had nobody helping me. I had no money and no nothing. I just ran right up into the mountains. When I was recaptured and they brought me back in, I spoke very freely about my ventures during those six days. It was something I couldn't deny . . . It wasn't a fear of conviction because I believed then and I believe more firmly now that I'll be acquitted. And not only that, I'll get a new trial on DaRonch. The irony of it all, Al, is it's probable the only solid conviction they will have on me will be the escape. Honest to God, I just got sick and tired of being locked up.

I kept saying to myself, Ted, in the event that you're acquitted here in Colorado and you go back to Utah and got a new trial on DaRonch, which I estimate would take three years. Even if we won at the trial court level the state would appeal and unless the Supreme Court overturns, we'll have to go to Federal Court. The Federal Court takes years and years and even if I got a new trial on DaRonch three years from now there's a chance I could be convicted on just the publicity of the whole thing.

I asked myself [if I were acquitted on all of it], could you go to law school? Could you go back to Liz? Would your friends be able to look you in the eye? Could you be Ted Bundy again? I figured, whether you're free tomorrow or you're free four years from now you're still going to have to make entirely a new life and really hide from the old life, whether legitimately or illegitimately. So, those are the priorities.

What a strange phone call. Ted said he just wanted to chat. (He likely called others as well.) Why? He said he wanted to know my impressions of his escape. His demeanor on the phone was like a teenage boy asking a friend of his impressions of his performance in a ball game. Again, it was my sense that I was listening to a lonely boy who needed to talk to a friend. I was surprised that he called me since my psychological assessment helped put him in prison.

It was clear from the phone call that he would again get tired of being locked up and he would try another escape if he found an opportunity to do so. He had accepted the fact that if he were ever freed or escaped again he would have to give up his family, his friends, and his career and start over in another country with a new identity. He was a person who kept track of everything around him. He watched for patterns of behavior. He remained friendly with everyone to throw them off guard for a possible escape. Then the opportunity presented itself and he took it.

Part II: The Interview

Introduction

There is much that we know about the life of Ted Bundy. For example, we have many facts about his childhood and his teenage years. We also are aware of some of his experiences in college, about Marjorie and Liz Kendall, and about his political activities. And we know the names of many of his victims and something about the manner in which he brought an end to their lives. Despite what facts we have, there is much more that is obscure about Ted's life. So I found myself asking, what if Ted had been willing to share his innermost secrets with us regarding the step-by-step development of his personality from the time he was a child until he was arrested?

This next section is just such a conversation. This speculative interview is what might have occurred between Ted Bundy and myself had he been willing to reveal himself to me. The information is taken from a number of sources including the initial testing and interview I had with Ted for the court in 1976, discussions with people who knew him, diagnostic interviews with other serial killers, and psychological assessments I conducted over a number of years of killers and sex offenders at the Utah State Prison. As such, it is my intention that this "interview" be as authoritative as anything of its nature can be.

This speculative interview takes place just prior to his execution.

Chapter One

Florida State Penitentiary

[The interview room is small, not much bigger than a prison cell, perhaps twelve feet on a side. As I enter, Ted is seated at a table. He doesn't rise—he is handcuffed, and a chain anchors him to the table. Ted wears a prison jump suit, and his hair is shorter than when I last visited him—but still not shaved for the execution. He looks tired, exhausted even, but considering that he is scheduled for execution the following night, there is still a twinkle in his eye. He smiles at me, and then at the guard, who is waiting to lock me in with Ted. I nod to the guard as I set up my tape recorder. The door shuts behind me.]

⁊

Ted, thank you for being willing to talk to me again. As we agreed, we're going to discuss how you became a serial killer.

> Well, I'm not sure what good it's going to do but I really can't see what I have to lose. I've been meeting with Dr. Dobson and other men of the cloth recently. I'm not sure if I believe in God but if there really is a God then I want to do everything I can to be forgiven for my crimes.

Most people would see that as an empty declaration. They would think that you are just trying to get a stay of execution at best, or even that this is a last ditch effort to salvage your reputation from that of one of the most evil psychopaths the world has ever known.

> Personally, I don't give a damn what the world thinks. If I get a last minute stay, I will be happy. If not, then I won't be around to hear people's comments. The only thing I care about, other than facing God—if in fact there is a God—is that my mother and family don't get harassed. They are innocent bystanders and I wish people would leave them the hell alone.

Tomorrow is your execution. How are you handling it?

> About as well as can be expected under the circumstances. As I told you in Utah, I don't worry about tomorrow. Fear of what is going to happen has never been a major issue with me. I have concern, mind you, but not fear.

Ted, have you actually killed a large number of women in the Northwest and in other states?

Well, ah, I still hate to admit it but . . . ah . . . yes, I did.

About how many have you actually killed?

I'm not really sure but it's, ah . . . thirty or more.

Do you remember them all?

Ah, I think so. Sure. At least most of them.

Thirty victims is quite a few. How is it that you can remember them?

I'm not sure I can really explain it. Death, and in particular, violent death, is a profound experience. You never forget what you saw or what you felt. In my case, the act of violent death bonded me to my victims. I won't tell you everything about each of them but each victim will never leave me.

What do you mean, bonded with your victims? If I was a parent of one of your victims, that statement would scare me to death.

As I said, I'm not sure that I can explain it. I'm not sure I want to. Maybe later in our conversation I'll try to tell you what I mean.

Do you feel you're ready to talk about them?

Many of them but . . . not all.

Why is that? Are you fearful there might be additional charges made against you?

Well, no, not really. I've already been found guilty of several homicides. (He laughs.) I don't think that one or two more would make any difference.

What is it then? Help me understand the reason you feel you can't reveal everything.

The connection I had with some of my victims is very personal. I don't want to talk about it.

It is about the ways you hurt your victims?

That's part of it but only part. I can't explain it right now but, as I said, later on I might tell you. Suffice it to say there is far more to all of this than anyone can understand.

All right. (I pause.) Society sees you as a psychopath. Are you a psychopath?

Well, some have classified me a psychopath and, according to the popular definition of that term, I guess I am. But you've got to understand, I don't see myself that way at all. I'm no different than thousands of others who are roaming the streets every day. To me, a psychopath is the used car salesman who feels no remorse after having cleaned out a widow's savings on a car that he knows is going to break down in a week. He knows it's a worthless piece of junk but he sells it to her anyway. He'll pocket her money and then go home to his wife and kids and tell them he made a good sale today. No, I may act like a psychopath in the eyes of society but this is a simplistic explanation of what is happening within me and other criminals in prison. There's a lot more that I and others could say about it but we don't because nobody wants to listen. They would understand the term better if they saw it from our point of view. Society has already made up its mind and doesn't want to see us as other than monsters with fangs and drool coming down from our mouths.

I think we could debate this term for hours but I'm not sure it would get us anywhere. The word out there is that you killed at random and I can't see that you feel any remorse over the death of any of your victims. That's why I feel you fit the criteria of a psychopath.

> Really, Al, what I've done isn't that different from what others do. How often do people brag about the prize buck or the bull elk whose head is hanging on their wall? I don't see how the taking of one type of life is any different from any other type. Life is life and animals are just as much alive as humans are. There's really no difference. Killing a human is no different than killing an animal. If it's all right to eliminate one type of life, then why isn't it just as permissible to eliminate another? Maybe these people with large mounts on their walls have some psychopathy in them as well.

Have you always believed that, Ted?

> No, it's a conclusion I came to as I got older.

Did life not have any meaning to you when you were a child?

> Yes, it did, but then I was just a child. I hadn't yet learned what life was all about.

What was so terrible about your life that you lost all appreciation for ethics and morals?

> Well, in many ways, my life was no different than others. However, there may have been some experiences that made me a little jaded.

Well then, tell me, where did you get that lust for killing? Did it come from your breakup with Marjorie?

No, not really. You alluded to that in the report you did on me for the court in Salt Lake. And, somehow, others seem to believe that as well. I can tell you unequivocally that it had nothing to do with my relationship with Marjorie.

Nothing?

Well, very little.

Marjorie was tall and attractive and her hair was parted in the middle and hung down the sides of her head. Many of your victims looked much the same.

At that time, most women looked like that. It was the style then. I selected my victims because I sensed their vulnerability, not because of any particular physical characteristics.

Well, Ted, where did the problem start?

I believe it started with my gaining an interest in pornography.

But most people who develop an addiction to porn don't become killers. Where did it really begin?

I'm really not sure. It's something that creeps up on you, like a virus or cancer growing in you of which you're not aware until you begin to experience some of its effects. But, even then, you don't think it's anything serious so you don't do anything about it. When you do begin to sense that there is a major problem, it's often too late.

Every virus has a beginning. Something enters your body and your body has to be vulnerable to it for it to take effect. The

Black Plague killed half of the people in Europe but still about half lived through it even though they were in daily contact with those who had it.

> Well, yes, but that's a physical disease. I don't see how that analogy applies to my case.

When researchers look for causes of serial homicide, they point to factors such as broken homes and physical and emotional abuse. However, the vast majority of children who come from divorced parents or abusive stepparents or even being teased in school never commit homicide, let alone become serial killers. What made you so vulnerable that the thought of killing could find a place in your mind?

> How much time do you have?

Well, if it's all right with you, I would like to explore your childhood again to see if there were any beginnings of psychopathy during that period of your life.

> But, as you've said before, a consistent link hasn't been found between a person's crimes and childhood experiences. Personally, I feel that nobody really knows why a person becomes a serial killer. It's probably different for each killer. Part of my problem, as I said, was that I got involved with violent pornography.

But many people do and they don't become killers.

> But, with me, I gradually got hooked on it and I wanted more and more. It reached the point where I wanted to experience the real thing and I kept trying to get closer and closer to it without stepping over the line. Then one day I went too far.

I would like to talk about what caused you to step over the line and why you kept on doing so.

Chapter Two

Early Childhood

Let's start at the beginning. I'll refer to notes I made when we talked in Salt Lake. When you were four years old—this would be sometime in 1950—you moved from Philadelphia, Pennsylvania to the state of Washington. What were some of your earliest memories of that time in your life?

> I still don't see how revisiting my childhood is going to do any good, but all right. I was too young to remember much about it. I do remember that after we settled in Washington I was lonely for my grandparents. But I had my mother.

Shortly after you arrived in Washington, she married and had other children.

> Yes but I don't see . . .

You experienced a loss in your life. First, you lost your grandparents, and then you lost your mother to your stepfather and, following that, you lost her again to your siblings when they came into the home. Ted, tell me something. It's been reported that when you were living in Philadelphia, you were told your mother was actually your sister. Is that true?

> I was too young to know much about that at that time. She was a good mother to me and that's all that mattered.

But could it have had an effect on your personality development?

> So your hypothesis is that I became a serial killer because I was told my mother was my sister? I admit my home life may have been dysfunctional, but even I'm not willing to buy that idea.

Many famous artists, writers, and actors came from very dysfunctional homes. Beethoven was severely abused by an angry, alcoholic father, for example. A dysfunctional home doesn't, in and of itself, generate a killing personality. However, unless a child has certain basic needs fulfilled, it very often leads to psychic hunger.

I remember an experiment I read about when I was in college. The experimenters underfed a group of mice from the time they were born and continued doing so through their juvenile years. When the mice reached adulthood, the experimenters allowed them to have all the food they wanted. As adults, the mice would eat and eat and eat but didn't seem to get filled up. They would hoard the excess food at the back of their cages until it went rotten and had to be removed by the experimenters. They concluded that if a mouse was hungry throughout its formative years, it had a very difficult time satisfying its hunger when it became an adult. Ted, you were lonely as a child, weren't you?

> You remember that I told you I had friends.

You told me about two friends before you started elementary school. You called yourselves the Three Musketeers. You said that was one of your happiest times as a child. However, something happened, didn't it?

> We lived in Browns Point at that time. Bill lived about a half mile away and Richard lived about two miles away. I was happy then, as you say. Then we moved to Tacoma, where I started kindergarten. I didn't want to move but I was too little to have anything to say about it.

You said your first grade teacher was a substitute who usually had a scowl on her face, and your second grade teacher put the fear of God in you by asking who in the class had been to Catechism that morning.

> Yes. I was afraid of her. I didn't know anything about the Catechism because I wasn't Catholic.

All right. Were you involved in activities with your family?

> Our family activities were always through the church. My mother worked as a secretary for our local Methodist Church and we went to church on Sundays and also during the week if there were any activities going on there. We would also visit with our relatives.

Did you have any friends when you were in elementary school?

> Not many. I guess you would probably call them acquaintances.

You were picked on, weren't you?

> To some degree, yes. We lived in an area where many of the kids were Italian Catholics. I didn't fit in and there were times when I'd run home from school so I wouldn't get beat up by them. But it was better after we moved from there.

Why did you move?

> The home we were in was too small for all of us, so after my second grade year we moved to a larger house. It was much better there.

Ted, I remember you telling me that you wanted to be in the top reading level in the class when you were in the fourth grade but you didn't make it. As I remember, you said you were "humiliated" by your failure. Humiliated is a very strong word, particularly for a boy who is only in the fourth grade. Why were you humiliated?

> We were poor and my clothes weren't as good as what the other kids had. And I was shy. There was this boy named Gerald whom all the girls seemed to like. They wanted to sit by him in class, eat at the same table as him in the lunch room, and I could hear the girls giggle as they talked about him. I used to watch the girls and soon I was able to discern who the popular boys were and what there was about them that made them popular.

Were you the only poor boy in your class?

> No. There was this boy named Ralph. It was pretty clear that he came from poverty. I saw how the kids picked on him and teased him. Nobody wanted to

sit next to him in class, and during the lunch hour he would get his tray of food and go sit by himself.

Would you ever go and sit by him?

No, I knew that if I did, the other kids would think that he and I were friends and they would also pick on me. I picked on him as well.

But you and he came from a similar level of poverty. You could understand better than the other kids that he needed a friend.

I refused to identify with him in any way whatsoever. I wouldn't allow him to pull me down to his level.

Ted, you already were at his level.

Maybe so, but I wouldn't allow myself to see it that way. I studied hard so that I would be able to answer the teacher's questions. Maybe I didn't dress as well as the other kids but, by God, I was going to be as smart as them. I knew I was intelligent and it was always a mystery to me why others didn't recognize it. As I got in the sixth and seventh grades, the other kids began to notice me more and I made more friends.

How did you accomplish that?

I was an excellent observer and I imitated the popular boys in some ways. I cut lawns and I saved my money and I bought clothes that were in style.

So, you became a pretender, an actor.

Yes, and it worked. I listened to all the radio serials and I practiced talking like the actors. This made the girls laugh and they told me how good I was at it. The other boys then seemed to have more respect for me. I was still a shy kid but when I was imitating one of my characters I had confidence. A lot of it. In junior high I ran track and I tried out for the football team. I even ran for class president.

I remember you mentioning it. But, as I remember, you didn't do very well in any of them.

I did all right in track but I didn't make it on the football team. I didn't have the right build and I hadn't studied the game well enough to be able to step in and play it with any degree of confidence.

What happened in the class elections?

They said it was a close race . . . but I lost.

When you compared yourself to the other kids in class, did you see yourself as like them or different from them?

That's a hard one to answer. Deep down inside, I felt that I was that inferior kid from the other side of the tracks, so to speak. I felt the other kids in class would laugh and make fun of me if they really knew who I was. I had acne when I was in my teens, which made it even worse.

As you approached high school, didn't you have a neighborhood group of friends who would get together and talk outside your homes in the evenings?

Well, yes. I felt very close to these friends.

With all due respect, Ted, when you were in prison in Utah we talked in detail about your childhood. Yes, you had some friends and there were one or two who continued to support you over the years, but I have absolutely no reason to believe that you were *close* to your childhood friends. The contact you had with other kids was within your own neighborhood and later they went their separate ways. In fact, when you were a child you spent most of your time listening to the radio.

Chapter Three

Effects of Loneliness

So you were lonely as a child because you didn't fit in with your family or with your peers at school but as you got older you had neighborhood friends. As I remember from our previous conversations, when you were in junior high, you started to come out of your shell. It was my impression that life was going better for you. What happened to change it?

> Well, first, I really didn't come out of my shell. As I have looked back on that time of my life, I did feel somewhat displaced by my family but I adjusted by creating my own world of fantasy and make believe. I also spent hours memorizing things I heard on the radio, not only the weekly serials but also parts of political speeches. I have always been interested in politics, even as a child. My fantasy

world was wonderful. In my daydreams I was a hero and everybody respected me. If I was interested in a particular girl in my class, I would bring her into my fantasy, and in that realm I was able to make her happy and that made me happy.

What affect did fantasy have on your self-esteem?

It allowed me to believe that I was important. I would imagine that I was rescuing a beautiful girl, or I would be giving speeches like some politician we studied in class, and everybody would come to me for advice. In my fantasy world, everything revolved around me. But, mind you, in the world in my mind I was always doing good for someone. I never hurt anyone. I never had a desire to hurt anyone.

Then all of this was normal for you.

Of course it was normal. Every child daydreams. I have every reason to believe that what I experienced was normal. There was really nothing about me that was odd or peculiar. If a person doesn't receive accolades from others for his efforts and accomplishments, he has to generate them for himself, and this happens in his mind if it doesn't occur in reality. If someone didn't see something the way I saw it, I felt they had to be wrong.

Let's talk about guilt. Did you ever experience much guilt?

As a child I did but I gradually learned to block out most of it. It's painful when you don't fit in. You feel that there is something wrong with you. You don't know what it is but you know there has to be something bad about you. My only defense was to create a daydream world in which I could do something heroic. When you put yourself in the center of your fantasies, everything is secondary to that. Everything you put in your daydream is to make you feel that you aren't inferior. Yes, I felt a lot of guilt and shame when I was a child but over time I became desensitized to it. If someone doesn't agree with something you believe in or they try to shame you for something you have done, then it's not difficult to find plenty of reasons why you are not as bad as they are saying you are. I didn't believe that I was God, mind you, but in some ways, in my daydreams, I was beginning to see myself in that light. I remember Christmastime when we would all rush to the tree to see what Santa had brought us. I didn't care what anybody else got; I was only interested in what was there for me. Me! My toys had to be better than any of the others. After all, I felt that I was more important than them.

Did you always see yourself that way?

No. When I was a little kid and I felt I didn't fit in, I compared it to a planet drifting out in space that didn't have a sun to orbit around. It's cold and lonely when you drift through empty space. You either have to find a sun to orbit around or you have to turn yourself into a sun and have others orbit around you. It may be all pretend but it's profoundly important that you do it.

Ted, it sounds like you were becoming self-centered.

I guess you could say that. But, at that time, I wasn't aware that this was what I was doing. I was just surviving and there was no one around to tell me anything different. When you are alone, as I felt I was, and you tell others that everything is all right, nobody has any reason to believe otherwise. It's like walking through a city of strangers. You take no notice of them, nor do they of you. Parents are wrapped up in their own lives. They are sincere and they care but they often don't understand what it means to *really* care.

I'm not following you. You have always said that your mother cared about you when you were growing up.

She cared in her own way but I was always able to hide my problems from her.

If you didn't tell her about the problems you were having, how could you say she didn't care?

She was busy with the church and with my siblings and she didn't take the time to talk to me. But remember, during the '50s and '60s parents were givers of advice. I don't believe they had any idea that their children were capable of having any deep emotional problems. I believe my parents cared for me but it was inconceivable to them that a lifelong emotional problem could be starting. Parents didn't listen to their children. The typical advice was always the same: Be a good boy and go to church; everything will be all right.

So you were very lonely as a child, and you felt that your parents didn't or couldn't care.

You're twisting common events in order to make it appear that my parents were the cause of my problems.

Not really. I believe your parents were good people who had high moral values and, like all parents, they raised you according to the best of their abilities. Almost all children have problems. It's just an issue of what they did in attempt to resolve them.

You said that as you got into junior high, you started to be more active in social contexts. You seemed to be saying that life got better for you. What happened to change it all?

> There were several things that happened, all within a short span of time, and I believe each caused my world—and in particular, my personality—to change. You can cover a dilapidated house with beautiful siding but underneath that siding is still an old home that continues to deteriorate.

But how does that apply to you? You were a young kid just getting a start in life. You had your entire future ahead of you. You were intelligent, you had a lawn cutting business which provided income and some degree of independence, and you were later able to buy some of the in-style clothes you wanted. Ted, a lot of people would say you had it made.

> The most beautiful flower will wither and die if you don't keep feeding it. Down inside, I was lonely and empty and I craved recognition. I didn't have the beginning of a confident identity. Without that, no matter how intelligent you are, you feel you are lacking and sometimes seriously so. There is no level of intelligence that can make up for that emptiness.

So what changed?

> Well, first, as I got into junior high and high school, there were fewer and fewer of my neighborhood friends who were around for our gatherings at

night. In high school everyone began going in different directions, some with sports, some with drama, and many with just the increased homework that was called for. I couldn't go into sports. I was too shy to take drama or debate, and I had no musical talent. I felt like that ugly child that nobody wanted to play with.

I remember you telling me that you began to date around this period of time. You even said you were enjoying kissing and petting but you stopped doing these things and you didn't go out on another date until your senior year in high school. What was your experience with the girls at school?

There was a girl named Gail Barker in my class that I was very attracted to. I often daydreamed about performing heroic tasks for her and, when I was about thirteen years old, I asked her to go get a soda with me. She turned me down. About a week later I saw her hanging around with a kid in our class named Devin. I was crushed. My daydreams had evolved from general heroic acts to specific exciting challenges in which I would incorporate pretty girls from school. In my mind I would risk my life performing the most courageous acts of heroism. I would look at a pretty girl in class and I'd keep an eye on her as I entered into a fantasy. The more dangerous the task, the more excited I became.

Really, these were some of my happiest moments. Sometimes a fantasy would last only a few moments but, if I was up in my room after school, I could stay in one for easily an hour.

What does this have to do with dating?

When Gail turned me down, I resorted even more to daydreaming. It was a wonderful escape. It was as though she had knocked me off my pedestal, and hearing the cheers of the crowds when I rescued the beautiful damsel in my mind put me back up on it. I knew the fantasies weren't real but that fact didn't change anything. I wanted them to be real, so I pretended they were and, after hundreds of times doing it, if I tried really hard, they sometimes were as real as if they had actually happened. You need to understand that the evolution of wishes into daydreams and from daydreams into deep fantasy was a very gradual process for me. It was slow and insidious but it was an escape and often profoundly exciting. It worked. I couldn't see anything wrong with it.

So what happened?

I got involved with pornography.

And that changed your life? Many boys dabble in porn but that doesn't turn them into serial killers.

Of course. It didn't turn me into one either. However, it can become the beginning of a process that if not altered can result in a damaged personality in a lonely boy who has no social skills. It hurt deeply when Gail preferred this other kid to me. Pornography was a substitution for a social relationship.

What form of pornography did you get into?

I came across a crime novel about a guy who kidnapped a woman and held her captive in his renovated basement in his home. I had been fantasizing to Reader's Digest stories about heroism but this novel was different. The story was about a man and his sexual pursuits.

Why do you think this novel was so important to you?

I was living in a crowded home in the city and we were poor. The villain in the book had wealth that came to him from a family inheritance. But at first I didn't see him as the villain. He lived in a mansion in the country surrounded by spacious landscapes. He was a bachelor, employed as an executive in a large banking firm. He had the type of life I wanted. He had respect, position, and wealth. I wanted what he had. I took on his role. In my mind, I imagined I was him.

The book began with the discovery of the deceased body of a woman, and then it cut to a profile of this bank executive. At first, I couldn't connect him with the murder. I thought that perhaps this was one of his girlfriends and I anticipated the book would be about the police helping him solve the crime.

But when the book got to the part about his basement and a woman he held captive there, I wanted to stop reading.

Why?

Because it destroyed my belief in him. In the mind of an innocent boy of that age, a well-respected banker who wears suits to work and is trusted by the public doesn't kidnap women and keep them locked up in a torture chamber because he needs sex. The concept was totally foreign to me. Sadistic rapists and bankers just don't live on the same planet. It just didn't seem right.

Did you stop reading the book?

No.

Why not?

Well, ah, it was new and exciting. It was a true mystery and I wanted to see how it would all come out. The guy was living a double life and I wanted to understand how he was able to carry it off.

But you were also living a double life, weren't you?

What do you mean?

You had this fantasy life in which you were a hero. You would rescue girls from houses engulfed in fire, or from devastating earthquakes. You were one person when you went to school and a very different person when you were living a fantasy.

But there was nothing wrong with that. I could control my fantasies.

But did a time come when you couldn't control them? A time when they controlled you?

Well, much later, yes but not then. I wasn't two different people and I wasn't developing multiple personality disorder.

Ted, why did you bring up multiple personality disorder? I wasn't suggesting that.

No, but others have suggested that I may have had a split personality.

Really, people have suggested many things about you. Why does this concept bother you so much? Didn't you speak of having an entity within you who, when he was brought to the surface, controlled your behavior? You even mentioned that back in 1975 when I did my evaluation on you.

> Honestly, Al, I have always believed that I had some type of a split personality, but I wasn't crazy.

What was there about you that made you think you might have a split personality?

> Well, there was nothing when I was a kid but over the years I began to create a separate part of me, and eventually this part that I had generated became formidable. I enjoyed it because it was more powerful than me in many ways.

You said that as a child you could control your fantasies.

> Yes.

But you chose not to.

> Well, at that point in my life, my fantasies were only about my heroic achievements. There was no need to control them because I had no concern about them. They worked wonderfully. It wasn't until later that they took on a violent theme.

Chapter Four

Pornography

Do you think that book had anything to do with the change from hero to violent themes?

> I didn't think so at the time but I later realized that my fantasies containing violence were only an extension of my hero fantasies. There was a beginning of a shift from encapsulating fantasy to believing these things could actually happen. This guy in the book wasn't just fantasizing about having sadistic sex with women, he was actually doing it. At least, that's what the author led me to believe.

> I was intrigued by the fact that he could have violent sex for hours at night but then was able to go to the bank the next morning and appear to be totally

normal. It was the most fascinating book I had ever read up to that time. I had a lot of respect for the person who owned the book and I felt that if it was all right for him to read it, then there was nothing wrong with me doing so.

You've got to understand, if I had read that book when I was in my later teens, it might not have had the impact on me that it did. But I was still a child, with a child's trusting mind.

Was it a relative's book?

I don't want to reveal who had it but when he was finished with it, he threw it in a basket of stuff to be taken to the garbage. I saw it when I was gathering up the trash.

How old were you when you found that book?

Oh, I was eleven or twelve years old. Fifth or sixth grade. I had been daydreaming about the hero, the disaster. I was waiting for an actual disaster to come but it didn't happen. At least, not in my life. I read those Reader's Digest stories again and again, and in my mind, I was there living it but there was no disaster in my neighborhood where I could be a hero.

Can you remember any of the stories you read?

Ah . . . yes . . . One of the stories was about a passenger plane that had crashed in deep snow in the mountains. I built a fantasy around it. I imagined that I was living in a small town in the valley below where the crash had occurred. In my daydream, I'm the only one with an understanding of that section of the mountain and the necessary experience to get those people out of there before they froze to death. My friends and the townspeople try to talk me out of it. They say that everyone is probably dead and I would only be risking my life by going up there. It would take at least three days to even get up there and back and a storm was coming in within two days. I know I may not make it in time but if I don't at least try, then anyone who might still be alive will die. I have to accept the risk because I couldn't live with myself if I didn't try. I'd rather die in the attempt than to have to live with the guilt I'd feel if I turned my back on them. When others tell me it's impossible for anyone to save them in time it just makes me even more determined.

Anyway, I get up there and I find some are still alive. As I'm giving the necessary instructions in preparation for the descent down the mountain, I notice a beautiful blonde girl sitting near the back of the plane. She is the most beautiful girl I have ever seen. She is hurt but I have to keep her alive. I can give the others instructions about how to follow me down the mountain but I know that this girl can't handle the dangerous slopes by herself. I carefully help her down the treacherous slopes and because she becomes so exhausted, I carry her the last two miles into town. Everyone cheers as we walk through town to the hospital. They call me a hero but I don't particularly care about their cheering. I only care that I have saved the life of the most

> beautiful girl on the face of the earth. I know that she will be mine forever.

You were really able to get into those stories. In fact, it seems you still can.

> Yes, and I did it again and again and again. Hundreds of times. I was somebody important in those stories, whereas when I put the Digest down I was back in reality where I didn't fit in. I would go downstairs to the boring conversation around the dinner table. I'd go out and talk to my friends, but for the most part I'd just listen. Then I would go back to my room and read another exciting disaster story.

I can see nothing wrong with the fantasy you just described to me. Many children have them. They are very normal. What happened when you found that book about the bank executive?

> When I first started reading it, I couldn't understand why a person would do such things. It didn't make any sense to me but here it was. It was happening. The feeling was, Wow, somebody actually did this. Print gives authority to a thought or an idea. It puts a validation to the whole thing. My daydreams weren't real because I was making them up but this . . . this was in print. To a twelve-year-old child, this was reality.

Why did it have such an effect on you?

> I had my first orgasm while I was reading that book.

Go on.

> It was the most intense, yet the most relaxing experience I had ever had. It was as though the weight

of the world had just been taken from me. Suddenly all the worries and concerns were gone. This was the answer to all my sadness. I lay on my bed and I felt so good. So good! This was the solution to all my problems. I didn't need to get permission to do it because my parents would never know. I could do it as often as I wanted. Now I wanted to know more about that book. This was the emotional component that was missing in the daydream about rescuing the girl in the plane.

Words in a book like this become translated into images. To adults, it's just another novel. Adults focus on the plot and on the characters. Children don't know anything about those things. They think in simple terms about simple things but they have powerful raw needs and emotions. If an adult doesn't feel he fits into a particular group, he has options. It's much harder for a child to see any options, so he is more likely to turn to whatever happens to come his way. That book came my way. I didn't go looking for it. It was there, on top of that trash. There were no pictures of naked women in it that might influence the owner to make sure a child wouldn't see it. People don't realize that, to a child, words describing a sexual experience can be even more important than pictures.

I imagined myself in physical contact with the girl in the book. I let the words build my own personal picture. In order to really get into it, I couldn't simply let myself believe that I was reading a book. I had to imagine that it was really happening, and by reading it again and again and focusing more intently each time, it came alive. I saw the room, the flickering light of the torch tucked in its holder. I was in the dark chamber with the banker, and this woman was illuminated by a light overhead. As the banker was running his hand along her thigh, I was right there with him, doing the same thing. The experience didn't go away when I put the book down. It occupied my mind and my thoughts to the exclusion of everything else for an hour or more after that. I couldn't wait to get back to that book to see what would happen next. It was surreal. It had a reality. Logically, I knew it wasn't actually happening but, emotionally, it was taking place. It's happening and I . . . it's happening . . . it's happening . . . and . . .

Ted, why did you stop just then?

I haven't thought about that for years. I don't think I ever fully realized the impact that book had on me. Actually, I had even forgotten all about it until a few years ago. At the time, as a child, I saw it simply as sex but that's not all it was. When I masturbated to those images of what he was doing to the naked woman, it was like injecting a drug into me that exploded into an intensity of emotion more powerful than could ever be put into words. All of my depression and anger and anxiety momentarily vanished. There was an incredible suspension of time when I stepped into the pages of that book. The only reality that existed at that moment was what was taking place in my mind. I felt more excitement and yet more peace than I had ever experienced in my life. It was absolutely earth-shattering.

So it became an answer to your problems.

Yes. Every time I was bored or upset about something, I came back to what I referred to as my solution. You're not so pressed to find another solution when you have one that is so readily available. So, sexual release through pornography was my answer to Gail not liking me.

I began wondering what girls looked like without their clothes on. I had never seen a naked girl before. I became very curious and I wanted to see. I couldn't see my sister naked, because my mother made sure the bathroom door was closed and locked every time she took a bath. I really didn't have access to any other girls around my age.

Chapter Five

Death of a Little Girl

Ted, when you were about fifteen years of age, a little girl who lived close by you disappeared. You had a paper route that went through her area. When I asked you about it before, you said that you had no memory of it having happened. I didn't push you about it at the time but I have always felt that you knew more about it than you were willing to talk about.

> What do you mean?

You said you were so involved with other things, it slipped by you unnoticed.

> Well, that's true. I don't remember anything about it.

Oh, come now, Ted. It was a huge event. It was in all the papers. I'm sure every family in the city was talking about it. Richard

Larsen, of the Seattle Times, told me there had never been as massive a manhunt as there was for that little girl. It would have been the dominant talk around school. Even your family, who knew you delivered papers to that area, would have asked you if you knew her. Ted, it's impossible for you not to have known about it.

> Well, maybe I did know about it but I don't remember much and I don't want to talk about it.

Is there a connection between the death of that little girl and Kimberly Leach . . .

> No!

. . . Other than the fact that both of them were young girls?

[Small beads of perspiration form on Ted's forehead. I don't know if it is the memory of Kimberly Leach that triggers it, or the little girl when he was a teenager, or perhaps both.]

> I won't talk about that one either.

All right. Let's assume the killer wasn't you. Let's assume that it was somebody else. You've become acquainted with child molesters and various other types of killers here at the prison, and I know you've advised the police on the motives of other serial killers. Would you be willing to make an educated guess about the person who might have kidnapped that girl?

> I can't see anything to gain in talking about her.

Humor me on this one. People often ask questions about the differences between adult and teen sexual offenders.

> Well, I guess I could do that, as long as you don't try to trap me into saying that I killed that girl.

I'll agree to that.

Well, based on the little bit of information I've read about it, if she was kidnapped by someone and it was not a crime perpetuated by a member of her family, I'd say the kidnapper was someone the girl knew and trusted. The perpetrator came by at night, as I remember. He may have told the girl that he had something very exciting to show her but that it could be seen only at night. He may have said that he would come by when everyone was asleep. He would wake her up and tell her he would take her to see it, whatever it was, and then they would come back and she could go back to bed. He might have offered her some candy, or he may have told her he had a baby bird or a small bunny to show her. He may have gotten her to agree to meet him and for her not to tell her parents. And if he had previously shown her some small animals or perhaps some pretty rocks, then going outside with him to see something would not necessarily have been entirely foreign to her.

Do you think he might have bated her before this night, or do you think this was a spontaneous act?

The fact that he waited until everybody was asleep and knowing that he would have to talk the girl out of the house would show it to be premeditated.

If it was an adult who kidnapped her, what do you think his personality was like?

If it was an adult, he would likely have been heavy into child porn. His initial intent was not to kill her but only to have a sexual experience with her. It was after he had molested her that he panicked. After he killed her, he would have buried her body somewhere. He wouldn't want the body to be found in case there was some evidence on her or at the crime scene that would implicate him.

Would he likely kill again or would he only do it once?

To kidnap a girl from her home at night is a very bold act. This would certainly not have been the first time he molested a child and, since he got away with it, it wouldn't be his last. However, it doesn't mean he would kill again.

If the perpetrator was an adult, would this kidnapping and death of the child make him stop molesting children?

Only for a short time. He loves children and he doesn't want to hurt them, so he would promise himself that he wouldn't kill another child. However, after some period of time, he would return to molesting children. He would tell himself that he isn't actually harming the child, or perhaps that after a little therapy the child would be all right. This is a psychopath.

I don't remember anything about child molestations in the area.

Perhaps he moved to another city soon after killing her.

How would the scenario have been different had this been a teenager who committed the act? Say, a boy about sixteen years old, for example.

Stop it! You're trying to get me to admit that I committed that crime.

No, I'm really not. I don't think you would admit to it even if you did do it. I'm trying to understand the difference in dynamics between an adult offender in cases such as this compared to a youthful offender and, since you lived in the area of this little girl at that time, I imagine that you have already given this some thought.

What if it was a teenager who committed the crime?

> Okay. (He takes a deep breath.) If it was a teenager, it would probably have been his first time at actually molesting a child. He would likely have been involved in pornography and he would have reached a point of wanting to interact with a real body. Pictures can only take you so far. He would have befriended the girl, not so much because he wanted to become sexually involved with her but because he just wanted to see what a girl's body looked like. He would not have come to kill her. He would have wanted to undress her and perhaps lie on her. He wouldn't have known that it would frighten her so much.

> He may have seen her with a bathing suit on running through the sprinkler. Since she seemed to like him, he could have believed that she wouldn't mind playing with him. He was unsophisticated when it came to understanding sex. When she started crying, he was afraid that someone would hear so he put his hand over her mouth . . . and . . . ah . . . after a while, she stopped crying. It took a few minutes for him to realize that she was dead. He didn't want to believe it. He didn't want her to die. She had become his friend!

If he didn't have a car, would he do it somewhere in her yard?

> Probably not. He wouldn't want to take the chance that her parents would wake up and hear them. As I remember, there was a park only a few blocks away. He may have taken her there.

> The boy would be profoundly affected by it. He may have developed an appetite for pornography but his fantasies hadn't evolved to the level of killing. The adult would likely seclude himself from the public because he wouldn't want people to notice him. The boy, on the other hand, would immediately get involved with activities at school and with his friends and his family. He would be devastated by what he had done and he would swear that he would never do it again. He might even hide his porn and not look at for a while. He would want to look as normal as possible. If he isolated himself, then he would appear different and people would wonder why.

How would he go about accomplishing looking normal?

> He tries to act normal in every way. He wouldn't want to believe that he's a killer and he is trying to not only convince others that he is normal, he's trying to convince himself as well. However, he's not, nor will he ever be, normal again. A change has occurred in him and he will never be able to go back to what he was. However, he doesn't yet realize it yet. The first thing he experiences is the fear of getting caught.

Because he's afraid that he will be locked up?

No, that's a secondary concern. He pictures the look of horror and shock on the faces of his family and friends. He hears them say, "You? You killed that sweet little girl? Oh, how could you have done such an evil thing?"

How would it change his personality and his belief about his future?

You need to understand, when an adult sex offender kills a victim, the act of killing isn't a total shock to his mind. His act is simply an extension of his fantasies. It's only one step beyond who he was prior to the act. He has already seared his conscience by then so his primary concern is about not getting caught.

Now, with the boy, that's completely different. He has hopes and dreams about the future but he doesn't yet have the personality or skills to carry them out. A person doesn't create an identity for himself. It evolves naturally according to his experiences. With having had the experience of killing this girl, he now has an identity burned into his brain of being a killer. It's a shaky identity, because he had no intent on killing her. He keeps telling himself that it was an accident. However, just as he can't make her live again in reality, he can't make her live in his mind. His predominant memory of her will always be of the look of fear and terror in her eyes when she realized that he was harming her. In her eyes he had rapidly changed from a friend into something very evil, and it's that thought of being evil that's implanted in his brain. Even though he keeps

> telling himself that it was an accident, he can't rid himself of the thought that maybe it wasn't.

So how does he begin to cope with it?

> He plays the event over and over in his mind, hundreds of times, trying to figure out what went wrong. Sooner or later he realizes that he had the choice of killing her or letting her go and risking the possibility that she would tell her parents. He realizes that, at that moment, his reputation was more important than her life.

But that's a psychopathic thought.

> Yes but it didn't start with that event. It had likely been gradually developing within him for years. If he's so desperate that he has to sneak out of his home at night to attempt to engage in sexual play with a little girl, then he must be very lonely. It suggests that he wasn't happy at home.

What do you mean?

> Most people can't understand what it's like to watch your mother laugh and play and show unbridled love towards a younger sibling and, when you try to get some of that love, you are brushed aside and told to go play outside. Because of this and other perceived types of rejection, the child may not have attached himself to his family, and if he couldn't find inclusion through family activities, there would be less bonding. Some children will act out to get attention. Some will withdraw into a shell.

But some will get involved with friends, school, sports, or perhaps music.

And if that happens, the child is all right and he's not likely to be doing this type of act. It's when it doesn't happen that it becomes a problem. The lonely child is like an astronaut hanging out in space, connected to the capsule by only a tether, and nobody notices him out there. If the tether breaks he may drift into blackness . . . forever. If it was a teenager who killed that girl it was because he was so wrapped up in his own selfish desires that he couldn't think ahead of what that little girl needed.

There's a problem with what you are saying. A child may feel detached from his family and friends but that doesn't mean that he will harm anyone, let alone kill someone.

That's right, but, under the right circumstances, any child can kill another person.

Let's come back to the possibility that a boy killed this little girl. If so, how would that change him?

Well, he would have to get rid of the body. Then he would have gone home and crawled into bed but he wouldn't have been able to sleep. When the news came out the next day about the girl being missing, he would have wanted to find out if the police had any leads. When groups were organized to look for her, he would have wanted to take part in the searches.

Why?

Partly because he wanted others to believe that he had compassion for the girl. But this isn't the only reason. He has become very confused about his identity and helping in the search was helping him to act—and to some degree temporarily feel normal. Also, he could be closer to the talk and to any information the police might have.

However, it would have its drawbacks. The more he heard people talking about how much they hated the person who did that and what they wanted to do to him, the more guilt he would feel. He would want it to all die down as soon as possible.

Why do you think he didn't just leave the body where it was? Why did he move it? How did he move it?

If he had the means of transporting it, he may have wanted to hide it just in case he had left any incriminating evidence on the body or at the crime scene.

But how could he have the means to transport the girl's body?

He is a teenage boy and she is a little girl. He could carry her somewhere.

Do you think he may have been listening to detective stories on the radio that would suggest this?

That's possible. Maybe he believed that if there was no body there could be no conviction, even if he did become a suspect. Also, if there was no body and no funeral, it would be easier to convince himself that it didn't happen.

Do you think the boy would have felt guilty about what he had done?

Well, of course. He would have experienced terrible guilt. Guilt is not only an emotion, it is a process. A person learns not to feel guilt about certain things but will feel guilt over a more serious misdeed. A teenager may feel no guilt over cheating on a test or for telling lies to his parents, but he may feel horrible guilt the first time he has sex. But if he and his girlfriend continue to have sex, they will feel it less and less.

So would it take a teenage boy long to get over this crime?

It would take him a long, long time to get over it, if he ever did. As often as possible, he would avoid situations that would make him feel guilt, particularly with religion. He would find fault with his church, including the minister and the parishioners. He wouldn't defy God, just in case there was one and he would be fearful of the possibility that he was going to hell, if there was such a place. He had already convinced himself to some degree that God didn't exist but he wouldn't want to take a chance.

For a short while, he would be paranoid. When someone looked at him in a strange manner, he would wonder if they suspected him. After all, he had a paper route there. Each time he would close his eyes and try to sleep, he would relive the girl's death all over again. The first couple of nights after the crime, he would feel the girl's spirit in his room and think that her ghost might be haunting him.

But everything would begin to die down and return to normal. After a few months he would be back to as normal as he could be at that point in his life. He would promise himself that he would never do it again and he would be quite sincere about it and, except under extreme circumstances, he probably wouldn't do it again.

But then, we come to another step in the psycho-pathic process. The boy would be proud of his repentance and he would tell himself that what he has learned is very valuable. But, at the same time, there is still another realization which had been creeping into his mind. He realizes that he even though it was an accident, he had gotten away with murder and the smartest minds in the police department hadn't been able to catch him. He begins wondering if he was just lucky, or if he was smart. He feels a sense of mastery and, over time, he may gloat over it. Remember, he had been feeling inferior but now he feels superior.

He learns to separate the victim as a person from the process of what happened. It was devastating that it was a little girl but it took an exceptional mastermind to get away with such a crime. Within about six months, or less, the whole thing would seem like it was a dream. An adult sex offender will sometimes take mementos from their victims but, in our hypothetical case of the teenage boy, he would not have wanted anything that reminded him of her.

This is another step towards becoming a psychopathic killer, wouldn't you agree?

Yes. He has seriously harmed someone, he has pushed religion and God out of his thinking, he has found that he can suppress feelings of guilt, and he has experienced exhilaration at outsmarting the police. He has taken a major step away from being a child with a conscience to a child who has started to train his mind to not feel guilt.

Then won't others see him as a cocky and self-centered person?

Not necessarily. If he is shy and lacks social skills, this act won't necessarily help him to improve these skills. And, remember, this act didn't eliminate all of his guilt. He learned to suppress it but a lot of it is still there, hidden deep within his mind. Guilt is multifaceted. But, if he didn't improve his life, the process of him being able to avoid guilt could become permanent. Then he could become a full-fledged psychopath.

Now, all of this is what I've learned from the inmates here at the prison. I didn't kill that girl.

Chapter Six

Teenage Years

Ted, when I talked to you at the Utah State prison, I asked if it affected you to learn that you were illegitimate. You said that it never bothered you when your cousin told you about it. Is that really true?

> Well, I'm sure you know it did bother me or you wouldn't be asking about it. Really, however, it wasn't that big of an issue.

But a girlfriend of yours said that you were extremely upset when you told her about being illegitimate. How did you happen to find out about it?

> I was about thirteen years old at the time. My cousin and I had been sparring over what each of us was going to do in the future. John said, "I'm going

to college and then I'll get an important job and I'll be rich." I countered, "Well, so am I. I'm also going to go to college and I'm smarter than you."

John said, "But I'm going to a better college. My mother is going to send me to college in Europe and I'm going to have a fancy car to drive around in."

We were really going strong on this and I couldn't let him outdo me. I said, "Well, I'm going to be famous too. I'm going to be more famous than you."

John countered, "No you won't. You won't ever be famous because you're illegitimate. You're a bastard. You don't even have a father."

That must have been very painful.

It was as if he had shoved a knife deep into my chest and then turned it slowly to intensify the pain. It didn't make any sense to me. I screamed, "You lie! You're a liar! I'm not illegitimate!"

John yelled, "No, I'm not lying. I saw your birth certificate in the old trunk in the attic and it said that your father was unknown. You're illegitimate."

I began crying hysterically. John could see that he had seriously hurt me and he quickly backed off from what he was saying. I had previously seen the trunk that John was talking about and I had asked my mother what was in it. I was told that it contained private family papers and that I was to stay away from it.

What did you do then?

I began running for the attic. John tried to stop me but my emotions were so intense that nothing could have deterred me from finding that birth certificate.

The trunk was there and it was unlocked. I jerked the lid open and pushed papers aside to find the one I was looking for. When I found a large envelope that had "Birth Certificates" written on the front of it, I almost tore the flap off. The envelope contained the certificates of each of the children in our family. I grabbed the certificate that had my name on the outside. I opened it and quickly found the slot where my father's name should have been. It said, "Unknown."

I had always understood that my father was dead. I knew what illegitimate meant because our preacher talked about it from time to time from the pulpit in church. An illegitimate child was shunned as if he was evil or some kind of a freak. I didn't know any illegitimate children but I knew that if there was one in my school I wouldn't want to be seen with him. I was suddenly aware that I was one of those things . . . those . . . bastards. It was clear why I had always felt that I was different from my mom's other children. They were legitimate children. I was the bastard child.

Did you ask your mom about it?

No. I cared for my mom and I didn't want to hurt her and I didn't want her to know that I had broken into the trunk after she told me to stay away from it.

Liz Kendall said that you broke down and cried when you informed her that you were illegitimate.

> I didn't believe that any woman would want to marry anyone who was illegitimate.

Did this have any effect on you eventually becoming a killer?

> I imagine it did to some degree. I had always felt inferior to others and I knew now that I wasn't the same as the other kids in my neighborhood or my class at school. I didn't want anyone to know about me being illegitimate and John promised that he wouldn't tell anyone. He kept that promise, and he and I have been friends since then.

> I think this was one of the reasons I set my goals so high on an important career. I believed that no girl could love me if she knew about it, but if I had position and money then it wouldn't be as big of an issue. I would have to keep my illegitimacy hidden from my children, though.

How did you adjust emotionally to this new discovery?

> I didn't allow myself to think about it. Like other things I didn't want to face, I turned to my hero fantasies and to masturbation.

Ted, did you have any thoughts or urges about killing when you were a teenager?

> Are you asking about thoughts of killing or urges towards doing so? You realize you're talking about two very different things.

All right, let's start with thoughts about killing.

> I had thoughts about killing but they weren't about me doing the killing.

Explain.

> I was heavy into pornography during my teens and I was also reading detective stories. The hero fantasies I had as a child evolved into fantasies about solving crimes.

But why . . .

> Every kid wants to be good at something. Some of the kids in my school were good in sports, some in music, and some in academics. Every boy wants a girlfriend, someone who will look at him as if he is worth looking at. I was a detective and a politician, even though it was only in my mind.

But you were good in academics. You also helped your friends run for school positions.

> I helped others run for school positions but they weren't necessarily my friends. I had only a couple of good friends throughout my high school years. Glenn was one of the popular guys in school. Everybody liked him. He was intelligent, had strong social acumen and he was a natural leader.

Did you spend a lot of time with him?

> Around him would be more accurate. He had a car and a few of us carpooled with him to school. He was accepting of everyone, and I felt that he allowed me to associate with him more out of kindness than anything else.

Did you feel you were the runt of the pack?

> Yes. I was not good in sports. I had no musical or acting talents, and there were no girls who looked

twice at me. People have made a big issue about my intelligence—you included. They point out my ability to pass my law classes at the U of U in Salt Lake even though I missed many of the lectures. However, I never did have much of an interest in the academic process.

But your achievements were almost always academic-related.

I wanted what a good education would bring me. It was the outcome I was interested in, not the process of learning. I did well in the classes that related directly to my career choice but not as well in others unless I had a strong interest in the topic or the teacher.

Is that why your level of achievement was on a B level in high school yet you obtained A grades in your psychology classes in college?

Yes.

Chapter Seven

Voyeurism

You spent a lot of time during your teens riding your bike or walking around after dark.

> That started earlier in my childhood. As I've said before, I was very comfortable in the dark.

You indicated in the past that you would look through windows in houses at night to see if you could see girls and women undressing.

> Yes.

Do you remember one of the first times you did it and the effect it had on you?

> My room was on the second floor of our house and it looked down to the bathroom of the house next

to us. I would sit in the dark for long periods of time hoping I would see something. There was usually nothing to see but occasionally I was able to see someone bathing through the misty window.

I had also been looking at nude female bodies in magazines and I wanted to see a live one so I decided to go to a neighborhood several blocks from our home. I wasn't sure if I had the courage to do it.

I walked several blocks from my home because I didn't want to take the chance of anyone recognizing me if someone saw me. I had planned very carefully about how to go about it. There had to be no street lights down on the corner just in case I had to run that way. I selected a small house that had big trees and shrubs around it. And a fence. There had to be a shrub-lined fence so no one could drive by and see me peeking in a window. I found the house. It was an experiment. Only an experiment. I wanted to see if I could do it.

I watched to make sure that no one was around and I climbed over the fence and then I crouched down to listen to see if there was a dog or anything. I was ready to jump back over the fence if I heard something. I waited a long time and then I began sneaking very quietly towards the light coming from one of the windows. It was a kitchen and I peaked in from the bottom corner of the window and I watched. There were curtains over the window but I could still see everybody. I stayed there for a long time because it was like I was invisible. I could see them but they couldn't see me. I liked being invisible. Some people would come into the kitchen and leave again. There was nothing sexual about it but, still, it was all very exciting and very mysterious. I know it doesn't seem very eventful to you but to a young boy like me it was a great accomplishment. It was one of the small turning points in my life.

It was almost midnight when I got home. My mom asked me where I had been and why I was out so late. I told her that I had been out playing Kick-the-Can with some of my friends and we were having so much fun the time got away from us. She asked if I wanted some dinner. She had saved some meat-loaf for me but I wasn't hungry. I went up to my room and I lay on the bed thinking of what I had done. I was so excited about it I couldn't sleep. As I lay on my bed, I couldn't believe that I had actually done it. And I started planning the next one.

Did you continue doing it?

Yes, and I got better and better at it. I never got caught.

Let's talk about something else, Ted. What were your high school years like?

I was extremely hungry for friendships. I knew I was intelligent but I didn't have the social ability to use it. I looked up to my friend Glenn. I wanted to be like him. I hung around him and his friends as often as I could, hoping I could learn by watching them. But I was invisible to them. It wasn't as if I was rejected. It was as if they didn't even know I was there.

I clearly remember one time when Glenn and I and another kid were walking down the hall in school.

> One of Glenn's friends came up to him and asked him and this other kid if they wanted to do something that night. This kid didn't even look at me.

That must have hurt.

> Well it did but I was used to not being accepted by my schoolmates. I just didn't know what I could do to make the situation different.

Ted, could there be any connection between the rejection you experienced in high school and the homicides you committed later on?

> Not directly, no. There was no single event in my life that caused me to kill women.

Do you still contend that your breakup with Marjorie had no effect on you beginning to kill?

> No. It's true that that experience was a primary junction in my life but it didn't cause me to start killing women. I wasn't prepared for what I went through with her and, in my attempt to adjust, I made some poor choices.

Chapter Eight

High School

But we're jumping ahead. Let's go back and complete your high school years. When I saw you in 1975, you told me that you weren't interested in social activities during your teens. You said, "I was just as secure with academic life. Social relations were not important." But they were extremely important to you.

> I was heavily involved with pornography by the time I was 15. That was my elixir, my retreat, my comfort zone. Porn and crime stories.

Had your fantasies changed by then?

> I was still into the hero fantasies but, instead of rescuing a girl, I was achieving fame through solving crimes.

Did you feel that there was anything inappropriate in this activity?

> No, Al. I didn't then and I still don't. As far as I was concerned then, my life was, for the most part, as normal as any other boy. Yes, I was very shy and I didn't have the courage to ask girls out on dates but I knew other boys who were just as shy as I was. I didn't see my fantasy life as anything more than a pleasurable game. I had no bitterness towards girls. Sure, I was envious of the guys who had the beautiful girls hanging around them but I knew that it was just a matter of time before I would have one as well. Even as I look back on it now the involvement with pornography was the only thing I would change.

How about your interest in crime novels?

> That was only a minor interest then. My primary interest was in politics.

Okay. Where did the interest in politics come from?

> I started becoming interested in politics when I was in elementary school. When I entered my junior and senior years of high school I helped other students with their political campaigns for school positions.

Were you good at it?

> Yes, quite good actually. It gave me some semblance of a social life. I was involved with campaign strategies, making posters, and in talking to other students about the candidate I was campaigning for. I got to know a lot of other students in ways that

wouldn't have been possible for me outside of a campaign. In fact, I asked a girl to go with me to the senior prom and she accepted.

How did it go?

Not well. I was very fearful of saying something stupid, so we talked very little throughout the night.

That must have made you feel even more awkward and inadequate, Ted.

Yes, it did.

Chapter Nine

Later Teen Years

When you were in senior high school, things were improving, weren't they?

What are you referring to?

The skiing.

Yes. It wasn't something I didn't anticipate.

What do you mean?

I knew that sooner or later I would find a way to fit in. I had developed a strong interest in skiing. I checked out every book I could find in the library on the subject and I bought my own skis and a ski outfit with the money I had saved from my lawn-mowing business. I taught myself how to ski. I was invited on a ski trip by some of the guys I campaigned for. I surprised them with my ability to handle the more difficult slopes. I even surprised myself because I was not shy around these guys up there on the slopes. They invited me for the next and the next . . .

You found that you could get a free ski card by changing the date on your tickets.

(Laughing) You remember that.

Well, of course. I used that as an example in my report to the court that you weren't as pure and clean as others felt you were.

But that was such a little thing.

Yes but it did help make the point.

I'd bleach out parts of the old tickets and mark over the old date with a new one. This made me even more popular because I'd do it for all the guys in our group. Unless you really looked closely you couldn't tell the doctored ticket was a fake. It saved us only a few dollars but it made an impression on these guys.

Did this activity change your life in any meaningful way?

Well, yes, as a matter of fact it did. It gave me some self-confidence. I knew I could fit in with the leaders of the school, and I was doing so on the slopes and in the lodge cafeteria and during the trip up and back. It felt damn good to have these guys look at me when they talked. The only other time I felt this good was when I helped in their campaigns. They included me in the school elections because I was good at it and I could help them get elected.

You didn't have a car of your own. You would borrow your parents' car but mostly you rode in the cars the other guys owned.

> We were quite poor and our family had only one car. I could use it from time to time but not if they needed it.

As I remember from our earlier conversations, there was something that went wrong about the whole skiing thing.

> You mean about the activities after a skiing trip, don't you?

Yes.

> There were times that they would talk about going to a dance or something that evening. They would go but I wasn't ever invited. It was the same with the campaigns, really. When it was announced that my candidate had won, it was followed by a victory celebration. I was always invited but at the end of the celebration the candidate elect would come up to me and say, "Thank you for your hard work on the campaign. I couldn't have done it without you. Your effort is really appreciated." He would then vigorously shake my hand as if I was his best friend. The next day I was invisible again. That's when I decided that someday I would be the candidate and others would work for my election!

Chapter Ten

Graduation from High School – Beginning of College

You told me once that your goal was set on finding a beautiful coed and having a career in politics. In fact, you gave those two goals in that order. Talk about that, will you?

> It was the beautiful coed that I really wanted but I didn't have the money to attract one. The political career would give me the position of importance I needed to attract the kind of girl I wanted.

You graduated from high school in 1965. What were your plans?

> The first thing I had to do was to earn some money and get a car. (Laughing) A girl doesn't like to walk to a dance. When I was a child I saw a movie about a lawyer who became a politician, and I was pro-foundly impressed. I had always been interested in

politics so I thought about a career in law. During the summer, I got a full time job and got a car. It was a reconditioned 1933 Plymouth Coupe. There was a guy who was campaigning for the House of Representatives and I thought this might give me a start in politics. This was something I understood. I got involved at night in the campaign, I was working during the day, and I was beginning to find myself.

Back then, people who saw me working in the campaign only saw a confident, outgoing person who would be voted most likely to succeed. They didn't see the Ted Bundy who was terrified of asking a girl for a date. I did well in politicking because it was structured. There were rules to the game, and if one followed the rules, had common sense, was good at oratory, and had a nice personality he could probably get elected. This was easy for me and I had no doubt that I could succeed at it. The rules of dating, on the other hand, were tenuous and ill-defined. They changed according to the personality of the girl you were taking out. Even if you did get it right on the first date you couldn't guarantee that the same rule would apply on the second date. Because I had a natural affinity towards political science, I could sit around a campaign table and debate with the best of them. This was the social environment I was comfortable with. Trying to hold up my end of a conversation with a single female was foreign to me.

Did you know anything more about sex when you started college?

My initial sex manual was that pocket book about the banker who kept a sex slave in his basement. After that it was the pictures of naked women I found in magazines in the library, then magazines at the bookstores such as Playboy. Sex, to me, was what these guys did in these stories. It wasn't about creating a loving relationship with a woman. Sex was love and love, sex. I didn't know the difference between the two. I knew that what my parents had was supposed to be love but that was a far cry from the exciting interaction that I read about in books—and which was alluded to in movies—between two naked bodies. Sex and love occurred when you overwhelmed a woman with your power. You were led to believe that if you kissed and touched her in the right way something would be triggered inside of her causing her to lose her will to resist you. You could then take her and do almost anything you desired to do to her and she would love you for it. *That* was my understanding of sex.

And on top of everything else, I had acne.

I know the acne bothered you. Let me ask you something else. Were you able to get any control over your pornography usage, or did you even attempt to do so?

I tried several times over the years to do so but it had become an obsession that I couldn't get rid of. When I became depressed, I had nowhere to turn. If I had a girlfriend that I could go to dances and movies with I would have felt normal. But I wasn't normal. Sure, I was able to help with high school campaigns but that occupied only a very small amount of my time. I went to the school functions but I always returned home alone. As I've said before, I was too shy to ask a girl for a date. Even at the school dances I stood on the sidelines and watched.

Was there anything different about your fantasies at this time?

They were the same for the most part. However, they were getting deeper and lasting longer. If I went to a game and then the dance afterward I often found myself staring at some attractive girl. Sometimes I would go home and continue thinking about her. Other times I would walk for miles through the city and I would be living a fantasy for much of that time. I couldn't give up my fantasy life because that's all I had. But I anticipated that it would shortly change.

Chapter Eleven

University of Puget Sound

After I graduated from high school, I started meet-ing people through the campaign and I felt that I was finally beginning to find myself. I had a small scholarship and a grant from the University of Puget Sound so I started college there. My parents had moved into a lovely old home located a couple of blocks from UPS allowing me to walk to school. I fully anticipated that my high school woes were behind me.

How did it go for you there?

The entire social scene was impenetrable at UPS. The majority of students were associated with the fraternities which was part of student housing.

There were very few students who were not part of a fraternity or sorority.

But you did go through rush for one of the fraternities, right?

I did but they wanted me to be full time in their program by the beginning of September. My full time job wouldn't be over until later in the month of September so I dropped rush.

Was that the only reason you didn't join a fraternity?

Well, no. I didn't have the stylish clothing or the social standing which would allow me to fit in with them.

So what did you do?

I went to my classes and then came home. I could connect with the students when I was at school, but at the end of the day they engaged in activities with their sororities and fraternities and I walked home and shot baskets, sometimes for hours. It was an extension of my high school trauma. I spent hours at a time walking. I loved to walk, particularly at night. It was my escape. It was peaceful and private.

You asked about my fantasy life. I still had hero and accomplishment types of fantasies. I loved watching people and if I saw an attractive girl I would construct a fantasy around her. Several blocks later when the fantasy had run its course, I snapped back to where I was and I'd realize that I had walked a considerable distance without being aware of anything other than what was in my mind.

There were times where I would be so deep into a fantasy that I could remember only parts of it when I came out of it. When I took psychology classes in college I learned about dissociation. I didn't realize it then but, as I look back on it now, I was dissociating when I was in a deep fantasy.

Ted, in the past we have talked about what you call an entity. Was it part of your personality when you were at UPS?

No, not yet. However, it was in its beginning stages of development. When I went out into the night, I was able to do more than just fantasize about women. I could pretend that I was stalking, looking for a woman. I would pretend that I was this gifted criminal, like I had read about in crime stories. Over time it became very real. People don't believe me when I say I was controlled by some form of something inside of me. I can't fully explain it, but it's real.

When did it begin to be a problem?

After Marjorie and I broke up.

You met her when you were going to the University of Washington. Right?

That was the beginning of the happiest period in my life but it was the most traumatic time as well.

Chapter Twelve

University of Washington

So it didn't work out at UPS.

> No. I became more lonely and depressed through-
> out that year. I still had a problem with acne but it
> wasn't as bad as it had been. I was very discour-
> aged but I still had great optimism that I could find
> that beautiful coed and a career. I decided to go
> to the University of Washington for my sophomore
> year. There was one good thing that happened dur-
> ing my freshman year at UPS, I sold my 1933 Plym-
> outh and bought a Volkswagen.

Ted, you mentioned an Asian student who you started dating
when you were in college. It seems that you haven't talked about
her to others who have interviewed you.

I didn't feel any need to do so. She was a factor in all of this but not a primary one. She was from Taiwan. Her family had moved to Seattle after the war. She was a freshman majoring in fashion design. She was very attractive.

What happened with that relationship?

When we were casually dating it was all right with her parents but when we started getting serious about a deeper relationship her parents cut it off. As with most Asian girls at that time, she had a very strong tie to her family and the cultural values and traditions of her ancestors. Her parents told her she needed to marry one of her own kind.

What affect did that have on you?

Not much, really. We had only been going together for a couple of months. There were huge differences in our lifestyles and I don't think that either of us seriously thought that it would work out. I was interested in Chinese studies and she seemed to fit in with that but I didn't ask her out with any serious intention of marrying her. It was disappointing in some ways but in another way it was very rewarding. This was the first girl I had asked out who was willing to go out with me for more than one date. It was a big boost to my ego because it allowed me to believe that girls could be interested in me. However, you have to understand that she wasn't just interested in me as a person. I was able to impress her with the accomplishments I was going to achieve in the future. I believe that she was more interested in my future dreams than in me. I was still incredibly shy but I had wonderful goals for my future.

Chapter Thirteen

Marjorie

We now come to a new development in your life. How did you meet Marjorie?

I met her on the ski slopes at Snoqualmie while she was waiting to go on the ski lift. She was a student at the University of Washington, a transplant from San Francisco. She was outgoing, tall, slim, and very beautiful. Her stylish ski outfit set her apart from the typical weekenders that populated the slopes. Her smile was unpretentious. Her carriage was erect, graceful, and had a rhythm all its own. She had a presence about her which drew me to her. I was emotionally starved at the time so her beauty struck me deeply. I couldn't take my eyes off her.

Talk about meeting her.

> I sat next to her on the chair lift and then followed her down a steep snowy decline. I timed my descent to make sure I would be next to her when she lined up for the lift and I struck up a conversation. When we reached the summit the second time I started down the slope ahead of her. I wanted to impress her with my ability to ski. I timed my descent so that I would stay just in front of her. She later said she was impressed by the smooth manner of which I was able to tackle a most difficult run.

It worked then?

> Yes, but I knew I couldn't continue doing this over and over again. She seemed intelligent and I knew she would soon catch on to what I was doing. I skipped the next run but I was waiting for her at the top for the run after that. She accepted my challenge for a friendly race down the slope. I had perfected the fine art of reading faces and body language and I knew that she wouldn't respect me if she won the race. I took the victory but I made sure I came in just ahead of her.

> She later said that she had sensed what I was doing but she didn't mind because I had a nice smile and I was a good skier. I told her I had transferred from the University of Puget Sound to the University of Washington to major in Chinese studies.

You were really trying to impress her.

> Yes, and it seemed to be working. I wanted to talk longer but she said she had to get back to her

apartment to work on a paper that was due Monday morning. I said I also had to leave to get ready for a chemistry exam.

Was that true?

No, but she wouldn't know the difference. I watched her as she first went up to the lodge and got some chili and apple pie with a scoop of ice cream on top. Then she left.

When did you see her again?

I spent an anxious week thinking about her. I couldn't understand why I was so nervous. I didn't believe in love at first sight, yet I couldn't get her out of my mind. I couldn't maintain focus in my classes or on my homework. I wanted to call her. I wanted to drive over to her apartment. I constantly found myself in a fantasy about her. Now she was the person I saved from that plane disaster in the mountains.

I went back to the ski resort the next Saturday and she was there. My intentions would be too obvious if I met her on the lift platform so I waited and caught the lift as she was coming down the slope. I then waited at the top until I saw her getting off the next lift. I pretended I didn't see her and, as she was getting close to me, I pushed off down the hill. I did this a few more times, always making sure she saw me, like a male peacock spreading his colorful plumes as he walked past a female of the same species. I got to the lodge before her. When she came in, I gave her enough time to take off her coat and, as she was walking towards a table, I made my move.

What did you do?

I walked towards her pretending not to see her. When I got close enough I acted surprised and said, "Oh, hi, Marjorie. It's good to see you again. How did you do on your paper?" She said she just eked it out on time, and she then asked me how I did on my chemistry test. I said something like, "I got an A on the test which gave me an A- for the class. Chemistry was never a favorite topic of mine. My forte is politics."

Was that true or was it a lie?

It was a lie. I hadn't yet taken a chemistry class, but my skill was in politics, so I guess it wasn't a complete lie. Why are you pursuing this?

Lying was becoming easy for you. It appears that telling the truth wasn't an important ethical principle for you. You were developing the traits of a psychopath.

I wanted to impress her and it worked. She said, "You must be quite intelligent to get an A- in a topic you aren't interested in."

"Well, I don't know about that," I said, "It's just that I need to get the best grades possible if I'm going to get into law school." She told me about her father's drive for success in business. She said, "Your ability to apply yourself is an admirable character trait. That's what brought my father to the position he is in now."

I scored and I had to make the next move quickly or I might lose her. I said, "Come have some chili and hot chocolate with me. I'm interested in hearing about your father. Maybe I could pick up some pointers that would help me in my career."

People want to be helpful and, when you ask someone to do something for you, they will often do it. I turned and began walking towards the snack bar before she had a chance to decline my offer. I listened for her to turn down my offer but she didn't say a word. I knew I had scored the next step.

She later informed me that she was impressed by my ability to take charge and make decisions. She wasn't aware that I had been practicing all week on things I might say to her if the opportunity came up to do so. She couldn't detect the fear behind my practiced smile. This initial move had gone well but it was only a beginning. I would have to make her believe that I was genuinely interested in her family . . . and I was. I couldn't leave anything to chance. My lines had been well rehearsed. It was as if I had spent hours practicing my lines for a play and it was now time to speak them. The curtain goes up. I enter stage right.

You have a clear memory of this event.

Yes. I have relived this hundreds of times. It's one of the happiest memories that I possess.

What did you do next?

I returned with the chili, hot chocolate, four napkins, water, and even toothpicks. Marjorie had found an empty table by the wall. I carefully placed the bowl of chili in front her, spoon on the right, knife next to the spoon with the cutting edge facing in, napkin next, and water above the knife. In a well-practiced British accent I said, "Here you go, milady. And when you finish with the main course I have one more surprise for your culinary delight." She laughed and, having said that, I returned to the snack bar and brought back two dishes of hot apple pie, each with a scoop of vanilla ice cream on top. While watching Marjorie the week before, I had noticed that she let her ice cream soften and begin to spread over her apple pie before she ate it, so I wanted to get it right away.

As we ate, I asked her about her father's business. She seemed hesitant at first to talk about him and I started to change the subject, but then she said that he was an executive of an international company. I was shocked. I felt that she had come from a family who was successful in business but not this. Although I wanted to know everything about him, I felt it was too early in the relationship to ask, so I changed the subject and began asking her about her college classes. I had about decided at that point that I had better back out of this relationship. If she came from a wealthy, successful family she wouldn't want anything to do with a boy who came from a poor middle class background.

But there was one other thing that was really bothering me as I listened to her talk about her life. I not only came from a fairly poor family, I was an illegitimate child. If she knew that she would have nothing to do with me. She would have walked away from the table without looking back. This conversation was scaring the hell out of me.

So how did she respond to you?

She acted as if she liked me. She began to telling me about her father, hesitatingly at first, possibly because she hadn't become well enough acquainted with me to know if she could trust me with this information. I was hoping that she wouldn't ask me about my family but I had prepared myself for such a question if it did come up.

And did it?

Yes. As I had anticipated, she did ask me about my parents.

And how did you get through that one?

I told her that I came from poor, hardworking American stock who valued education and achievement, and she seemed to accept that. For the most part, however, she was interested in my aspirations. I explained that I was going into law and politics and I was determined to fight for the poor and to help bring an end to discrimination. She asked why I was majoring in Chinese studies. I explained that I wanted to help improve the relationship between our countries. It turned out that she was interested in many of the same things.

"How are your classes going?" I asked.

"Oh, fairly good," Marjorie said, "except for my poly sci class. I have to write a position paper on the Communist Party in China."

I found that I could read Marjorie quite well. I felt she was sending a message that she needed help with her paper but was too proud to allow someone to write it for her. This was an opening I couldn't pass up. I had already lost one girlfriend—the Asian girl—and I didn't want to lose this opportunity if I could help it. I had dreamed about a woman such as this. This was the beautiful coed I had yearned for since my early teens.

So you made a play to help her?

"Look," I said, "I have a light day at UW tomorrow. I'd be happy to meet you at the library. I can show you some articles on both sides of that issue. China is a powerful nation and I really feel that we need to establish diplomatic ties now in order to ward off serious problems with them in the future. When I get my law degree I'm hoping to work my way into a position with the State Department. I either want to be an ambassador to China or I want to help right the wrongs of the poor in America. I grew up in relative poverty and I know what it's like to go without."

The conversation continued through the meal and she agreed to meet me in the UW library the next day. The agreement made, I cleaned off the table and said goodbye to Marjorie. Exit stage left.

I assume you did meet her.

Marjorie and I met the following day at the University of Washington Library. I helped her with the information she needed for her paper and then we went out for a bite to eat. As I look back on it now, I can't see that the relationship ever had any chance of succeeding.

Why is that?

I had a tan Volkswagen; Marjorie, a red Mustang. My clothes were those of the poor college student. She dressed and moved like something out of Vogue. I was poor and often didn't have enough money for gas for my car. She was wealthy and we often used her car.

Did you have anything in common?

I had an incredible dream of profound future accomplishments and she was looking for someone like that. I was able to convince her that I could achieve it. I acted as if I was more interested in my dream than in her money and this impressed her. I had already been involved in a political campaign and she said my eyes lit up when I talked about how much I enjoyed it. I was well versed in American and international politics and I could talk about it for hours. She said she could see some of her father in me.

So from what you are saying, I can see why she was impressed with you. What did you need from her?

I'm not sure what I needed from her except that she was beautiful.

You needed Marjorie, not only because she was so beautiful but because she was at a much higher station in life than you. You wanted to dress like her, drive a stylish car like hers, have a wide range of political and business contacts like her father had, and have people look at you with the respect and admiration you could see in their faces when they looked at Marjorie. Does that sound about right?

> So what's wrong with that?

Nothing if it works.

> Whenever Marjorie and I went anywhere people treated me as her equal and I did want to become like her. As you said, I wanted to wear stylish clothes, own a beautiful convertible, and have the wealth and station that she had. I fell in love with all of this but, most of all, I fell in love with Marjorie because Marjorie was the first woman who had ever, ever looked at me the way she did. Some of the happiest times I had with her was when I could show her off to my friends.

But I'm not sure if it really worked in your favor. It sounds as if you had to plan everything out. There was no spontaneity on your side of the relationship.

> I couldn't take any chances of losing her! My social skills with girls were never good and it was imperative that I made a positive impression. I was terrified of getting caught off guard by a question I wasn't ready for so I planned for every contingency so I wouldn't look stupid.

Ted, when I conducted my assessment of you for the court in Utah, I noticed that you did this. A couple of times when I asked you a question that I thought you probably weren't prepared for, you hesitated for several moments before you answered and, when you did, your response was far less applicable. Can you see the problem you created for yourself by doing this?

Well, no. Not really.

You never gave yourself a chance to be spontaneous. You never learned that people could like you for who you were. You were phony and you were always performing as if you were on stage. Also, you were developing a technique you would use in the future to stalk and con your victims. It was mind chess.

Hold on. What do you mean by mind chess?

It's a chess game, only it's carried out between two persons' minds rather than on a board. It's one thing if both you and the other person are aware that it is a game. However, if you use it on another person and she believes that what you are saying is honest and sincere, then you are deceiving her.

I don't agree with you that it was a game.

Ted, look at it this way. When you play this game, you size up your opponent and open with a move that allows you to get an idea of how she is going to play the game. Each time she gets ready to move one of her mental chess figures, you think of three counter-moves. No matter what she says or does, in your mind you are three moves ahead of her. In this way she can't do or say anything that you are not ready for You used it every time you kidnapped and killed a victim.

I was tired of being humiliated! My only intent was to win this girl over and, to do so, I had to appear intelligent and confident.

But your confidence was not genuine. It wasn't real. You were not becoming assured in who you were, only in your planning ability. You were attempting to structure the outside world to fit your fantasy world. In your fantasy world everything worked out according to your direction, and you believed that you could structure activities in your external world which would produce the same results. You experienced social anxiety and you felt unlovable so the result was a loss of spontaneity and flexibility. You wrote a script in your mind and you attempted to put it into action, hoping it would work out in reality.

> Being with her was surreal, like a dream, and I was afraid of even the slightest thing going wrong to make the dream end. You talked to Marjorie. You could see what she was like.

I only spoke to her over the phone but I felt she was an intelligent and confident person. As I saw it, the two of you were mismatched. You fell in love with her beauty, her status, her mature personality, and her wealth. She fell in love with your dream of the future and your ability to express it. She was fascinated with who she thought Ted was. She saw future greatness in you. You, on the other hand, were in love with her love. You were a love-starved child who craved passion. She wanted future. You wanted immediacy. She wanted conversation, spontaneity, adult debate, and someone who could stand up to her in an argument. You were immature, unpracticed in the conversational arts, and when confronted you would cower into passive acquiescence. She was genuine. You, on the other hand, were a well-practiced stage performer who, in the beginning, was able to carry it off fairly well. She enjoyed being with you but she wasn't obsessed with you in the way you were obsessed with her. You had to possess her, to own her, to keep her forever at your side for only then could you ever become someone important. She could fall deeply in love with you if her initial impression of you became reality. If not, her interest in you would die.

Chapter Fourteen

Stanford University, Summer 1967

You went to Stanford University in the summer of 1967. Why?
What happened there?

I enrolled in Chinese studies at Stanford because
of the noted superiority of their program. For a
short time, it was *the* high point of my entire life.
The relationship between Marjorie and me was going very well at that point. The campus was beautiful, the instructors magnificent, and my confidence
was very high. The environment was conducive for
learning. I did well in my classes and I had friends
that I played tennis with in the evenings or on week-
ends. The professors had exceptional knowledge
and experience and I loved listening to them. My
one regret was that Marjorie had remained back

at the University of Washington in Seattle for the summer in order to complete some classes that she needed towards her college degree. I tried to talk her into coming back to California for the summer but she wouldn't do it. I wasn't exactly terrified of her but I was fearful that this wonderful thing I finally had wouldn't last.

And problems began to occur?

Marjorie and I had been having a few squabbles over small things and we were becoming more distant from each other. Not only did I want to attend Stanford because of the superiority of their Chinese program, I wanted Marjorie and me to have the summer to develop our relationship. I was very insecure about losing her so I called her almost daily. This started to irritate her.

Everything began to deteriorate. Not all at once, mind you. Little things frightened me, such as a lack of enthusiasm in her voice when we talked. She got angry more often and for insignificant things such as when I locked my keys in my car. It bothered her when I forgot to pick something up at the store that she had wanted.

I didn't like it when it was always me having to call her and not her calling me. It began to wear on me. I couldn't focus on the instructors in class. I didn't complete my homework. I had been playing tennis but I was too anxious about Marjorie to do well at it. I went to a guest lecture on Chinese protocol which was usually of great interest to me. However, I took only a half-page of notes, a pitiful account for a two-hour lecture. As soon as it was over I ran back to my apartment and called Marjorie, but she wasn't there.

I walked around campus for a few hours and then I tried Marjorie again but she still wasn't home. I began to panic. I wanted to drive up there and talk to her. I had to make sure that everything was all right.

I went to the campus cafeteria and ordered a Coke and a ham sandwich. When I sat down at one of the tables I noticed an attractive dark-haired girl sitting at another table talking to a rather homely looking guy. This girl kept her eyes on the boy as he talked; her affection towards him was apparent. It nauseated me. I threw my empty Coke bottle and half-eaten sandwich in the garbage and left.

I walked around campus for a while and returned to my apartment around 8:00 pm. I again called Marjorie but she still wasn't there. I watched some TV but I couldn't keep my attention on what I was watching. About 9:00 I called Marjorie again but, still, she wasn't back at her apartment. I was scared. I put on dark cotton slacks, a dark turtle-neck sweater, and I went out for the evening.

As I walked around campus, I looked carefully at every girl I saw as if one of them might be Marjorie. There was one girl in particular that I came up behind who looked like it could have been her. I grabbed her and pulled her around. She had this terrified look in her eyes. I didn't know what to say.

I told her I was terribly sorry, that I thought she was someone else, and I left.

I hurried back to my apartment and began calling Marjorie again. I called every few minutes until about 11:00 pm, at which time she finally got home.

I didn't want to let on that I was so anxious.

"Hi Ted," she said, "How was your day?"

"Ah, it was all right. I played tennis with Gary Palco and I attended a lecture on Chinese customs."

"How was it?"

"Very interesting. Very interesting! I gained a new perspective on the problem between China and our current administration. I can't wait to get my degree and apply for a job in the Foreign Service."

"Well, that's good, Ted."

"How are you doing Marjorie? I've been trying to get in touch with you but you haven't been home."

"Well, I've been pretty busy, Ted. I'm trying to get these classes out of the way so that I can finish up here and come back home."

"Yeah, well, ah, I can see that. I've just been really missing you, that's all."

"But Ted, you know I have to get these done. I can't drag this out forever."

"I was just wondering where you were. I've really been missing you. It's just not the same here without you."

Marjorie said, "Ted, it's all right. I'll be home next week for my birthday and we'll spend some time with my parents and go out to dinner or something."

"Yes, all right. I was just thinking about you when I was playing tennis with Gary today. Have you had the chance to play any tennis up there?"

"Yes, I have. There's a student in one of my classes whom I've had a few games with."

"Oh . . . well . . . ah . . . that's all right. I called because I was concerned and I just wanted to make sure you were all right and ah . . . "

"Ted, don't worry. Everything's fine. Well, I've got to go. I'm working on a midterm paper. I'll be home next week and we'll do something fun. All right?"

"Yes, okay, I'll call you tomorrow. Will that be all right?"

"Yes, call me around nine tomorrow night. Judy Burgess, a friend of mine, wants to go out to dinner and I've got a few things after that I need to take care of but I should be home by nine."

When I put the receiver on the cradle, my hands were shaking. I couldn't account for the lack of enthusiasm in her voice and this frightened me. I had to go out again.

Chapter Fifteen

Deterioration

I got home about 2:00 am, somewhat relieved but still depressed. I remember putting on Beethoven's Third Symphony, which generally brought me out of a depression, but tonight it wasn't working. I didn't sleep hardly at all that night.

For the next few days I attempted to keep up my enthusiasm for the Chinese program. I reminded myself about the wonderful opportunity I was having to learn from professors who were so well grounded in their knowledge of foreign affairs. After all, this was Stanford University, one of the elite campuses in the country, and I was exceptionally lucky to have been accepted into the program in the first place. This was my future career.

I felt as if I was a home which had been built for a special purpose but now the foundation was deteriorating. The paint was coming off the walls. The cement was cracking and cold; dank water was seeping in.

That's a strong analogy. You *were* terrified.

I had a very difficult time adjusting to the school regimen the following week. A day without Marjorie was endless. The classes dragged. My mind constantly wandered, and when a professor said something interesting my focus would peak only to subside quickly when my queasy stomach distracted me once again. I later learned from my psychology classes at the University of Washington that lost love is unfinished business and I was becoming fearful that I might lose her. It disturbs the mind. It forces the psyche to seek immediate compensation. Order must be reestablished and safeguards must be erected to assure that imbalance won't happen again. However, the immediate balancing of my system was impossible. I couldn't keep fear from my mind.

What did you do about it?

Each night I fought the urge to go out but it was my only safety. I felt trapped in my dorm room, claustrophobic. Two of the things I loved the most were intense classical music and the freedom I felt out in the night. The night, to me, was like powerful music. I was at peace sitting on grass that was still warm from the daylight. I loved the feel of a cool breeze on my skin coming from the direction of the ocean. It was like listening to the Violin Concerto by Brahms. When I saw a beautiful coed walking arm in arm across campus with her boyfriend it was like a symphony by Beethoven. Peering through a window at a woman undressing for a shower and sensing my hands gently caressing her young breasts was Wagner.

Were you not unaware that window peeking was seriously amplifying your problem?

But it wasn't a problem. At least I didn't think so at the time. Apart from the pornography, it was the only defense I had against my depression.

You spent a lot of time going out at night window peeking. What did that do for you?

It was a way of bringing some reality to my desire to make love to someone. I still had my pornographic material but it was only part of the answer. When I had an intense desire for sexual release I needed something that was more real than pictures.

So what was it about going out at night that made it different?

The night was secret. It was powerful. There was a reality to my fantasies out in the dark night that was beyond anything that I could feel sitting alone in a small room. You've seen these movies where an attacker is sitting on a ledge watching the enemy walking below him. They don't know he's there and his position of being above them gives him the advantage. It's a point of power. One moment you are a small child crying in a confined room. The next you are a powerful superhero—or super villain.

Did you sense any need to stop?

> At times I did but this was mostly after an adventure into the night.

> I attempted to curtail my window peeking as much as possible out of fear of getting caught and arrested and of getting kicked out of school. It frightened me that I was beginning to lose myself in my fantasy.

> You asked about the Entity. One night when I was very stressed, I drove several blocks from the campus, parked my car, and I began walking through the backyards of the homes in the area. I came to one particular house in which a very beautiful girl was undressing for bed. As I watched her, I entered effortlessly into a dream. In my mind I was there with her! Inside her room! I was embracing the woman's naked body. Honest to God, Al, I could feel the warmth of her body in my hands. My hands had the sensations of feeling her body. I got so caught up in this image that for a few moments I completely forgot where I was, and this bothered me.

Why did this bother you?

> I had been aware for some time that there was something happening to me when I was peeking in windows. I had no fear of getting caught but, still, I was uneasy about this process that was taking place within me.

What was it that was happening?

> Al, there was a strange presence building within me that craved the dark of the night. It had started sev-

eral years back but, at that time, it was pure and sweet. I recognized it when I was deeply involved in a hero fantasy. I seemed to transform from my normal self into that other person. Like that fantasy where I rescued that beautiful woman from the plane crash in the mountains. I wanted to be him so badly that I laid on my bed in the dark and I pretended that I *was* him and . . . I was there. I could feel the cold of the snow and I began shivering. I jerked when I hit a branch. I grabbed the side of the bed when I slipped on a rock.

The more I repeated this process the less I was satisfied with simply thinking about it. For a fantasy to have the greatest impact, I had to find a way to be there, experiencing it. But I knew I couldn't go into the mountains to rescue a beautiful girl. Still, I could watch a woman undress. As I practiced projecting myself into a fantasy, I began to feel it, as though it was happening.

It sounds like fantasy was very adaptive at this point in your life.

Yes, it was, and my ability to achieve this level of separation gradually grew stronger, but only by small increments. I was pleased that I could create this process within me, and it became easier to do over time.

At first it was as if I was acting a part in a play. That is, I was playing the role and I was fully aware that I was only acting the part. But, as I began creating a more intense, powerful personality in this fantasy, I put every effort into sensing this part. In the beginning, the demarcation between me and the part I was playing was clear. I could be me playing the part or I could be this other person who was living the part. I was never both at the same time, and I had complete control over which I chose to be—it or me. Over time, however, the line of separation became cloudy and it was more difficult to discern if it was me or him that I was feeling.

Did this bother you?

No, not at first. It was fun. This thing was becoming different from me. Stronger, more devious, more cunning. That was all right with me because it gave me added power and confidence.

Regarding that fantasy about the girl in the mountains, I couldn't succeed in rescuing that girl under those dangerous circumstances if I allowed myself to be the timid, inadequate boy in junior high. I had to generate within myself the strength to accomplish the feat. Again, to a lonely and self-conscious boy, it had a level of power that I could attain in no other way than through fantasy.

Prior to that night when I was looking at that girl undress, I could control it. I didn't want to give it up because it was this process that allowed me to sense a reality that I needed so desperately. The distance between me and this girl suddenly collapsed and I was no longer outside a house watching it happen. I was inside the room. I was undressing her. I loved it. It was very satisfying to feel it. Then I would go home and masturbate to that memory. It was

> my release from stress. The only thing I didn't like about it was that when the process had completed its cycle and I was back to reality; while I felt some emotional satisfaction I also felt greater loneliness.

Your fantasy life was clearly getting out of hand. What impact did that have on your relationship with Marjorie?

> Well, it certainly didn't help. It made me want her all the more.

Chapter Sixteen

Marjorie's Birthday

You saw her again that summer didn't you?

Marjorie flew home to California for her birthday and her parents invited me to stay overnight at their residence rather than to have me drive back to Palo Alto following Marjorie's birthday celebration. Her father was a vice president of an international company making business machines and his company had hubs in France, England, and Italy. He had a shrewd business mind and he hoped his daughter would follow in his footsteps. He wanted grandchildren whom he could place in various parts of the world to watch over his holdings. He wanted to have some say about who Marjorie would marry but he had raised her to be independent and to make her own decisions.

He was very close to his daughter as was she to him and he encouraged her to make up her own mind about things. I was very impressed with him but I was very uncomfortable in that setting. I hadn't had enough experience to give any depth to my ideas. Life to me was like a game of chance and I functioned best when I was able to plan my moves.

I didn't know how to talk to him. Just imagine how difficult it would be for a second-year college student to attempt to carry on a meaningful conversation with a third-term United States senator. It was that difficult. They were warm and unpretentious and they invited me into their home with dignity, but I was unable to show any spontaneity in our interactions.

However, I don't want you to believe that I was completely out of my element. I was up on local and foreign politics. Because of my work in the political arena I was able to carry on a conversation, at least at some level.

How was the birthday celebration?

The birthday party was a lot of fun but I felt humiliated when I had to give Marjorie my small inexpensive gift following the luxurious gifts given to her by her parents.

To better understand what it was like in that environment, you need to consider the style of their home. The bed in the room I was given to sleep in had clean white sheets, a bedspread tucked in carefully at the corners by the maid, decorative lamps on each side of the bed, and hardwood bookshelves on the far wall with an ample variety of old classics, historical novels, and current thrillers for a guest to feast upon.

The next morning at breakfast I was given a poached egg cradled in a container which rested on a large gold-rimmed plate. There was a knife and spoon set meticulously on the right side of the plate, two forks on the left, and a butter knife located at the top of the plate. A linen napkin was folded neatly to the left of the forks and a small plate with buttered toast was placed above the napkin. All of this was foreign to me.

The next day Marjorie and I were scheduled to play some tennis. When Marjorie came down the stairs she was wearing a short white cotton skirt with a matching top. Sunlight from the window reflected off her face producing a glow as beautiful as anything I had ever seen. She was trim and very lovely and I wanted to throw my arms around her and tell her how much I loved her.

We went to the courts for a game of tennis but I was too tight and not up to my usual competitive skill. I told her my muscles were sore from a new exercise system that I was trying out.

We went back to the airport that afternoon for Marjorie to catch her flight back to Seattle. I tried to talk her into staying another day or two but she wouldn't. When she kissed me goodbye it didn't have the passion that I was used to. I watched her walk down the tarmac to the awaiting plane. I couldn't leave until the plane was out of sight. I watched it get smaller and smaller until it was a tiny speck silhouetted against the clouds. Then she was gone.

As I left the airport and got onto the freeway, I couldn't hold my thoughts together. I remember that it was close to sunset. I became very angry, not so much at Marjorie but at everyone. Vehicles seemed to come from out of nowhere, hurrying somewhere, filled with faceless people chatting about nothing meaningful. Empty words and hollow laughter emanating from brains programmed for superficial conversation; mindless sheep driving expensive cars, laughing and having fun.

The next couple of weeks were devastating. I attended fewer of my classes, my grades dropped, and I put less time into my preparations for class. Some days I was still able to pull it together and pass my exams but much of the time I just sat in class with an empty mind. Or I would walk aimlessly around campus. I played less tennis, made excuses for not attending the student parties, and began to avoid people. My need for pornographic material increased greatly and I was masturbating several times a day, but even that wasn't working for me.

Marjorie didn't return my calls as often and, when she did, she seemed to be making excuses to keep the conversation short. When I attempted to bait her by expressing my deep love for her, she didn't reciprocate my affection. When I tried to speak enthusiastically about my dreams of working for the government, she simply responded, "That's nice Ted. I hope you do." All of her statements were "you"—never "we" or "us." It was clear to me that the relationship was dying.

Chapter Seventeen

End of a Relationship

I became desperate. I couldn't sleep and, when I did, I had fitful dreams. Other students were asking what was wrong and offering to help in some way. One student suggested that I return to Seattle and work it out with Marjorie. I didn't want to do that because I was afraid that any pressure on her might bring a quick end. At first I decided to allow her time to think things over. However, I became more and more depressed and I didn't want to delay the inevitable, if it was going to go that way.

I flew up to Seattle and took Marjorie out to an exclusive restaurant. I needed to determine what was wrong so I could change it.

"Ted, please don't," she said. "Let it go. I'm sorry. I don't mean to hurt you but I just don't want to keep going on with this relationship. You're not what I need right now. I'm just not ready to settle down."

I couldn't think of anything to say except that I was sorry, too. "Tell me what's wrong," I said. "Whatever it is, I'm sure we can fix it. I need this relationship and I need you. I love you. I love you!"

She was exceptionally beautiful that night. I kept looking into her eyes for some indication of sympathy, some show of love, but there was just nothing there. Rage began to build within me. I didn't want her to see it so I turned away. I had always been there for her. I had gone to Stanford for her. She was the most important thing in my life. She owed me more respect than she was showing me.

She reached over and put her hand on mine. "Ted, I admire you," she said, "and I believe you have a good career ahead of you. I don't want to ever lose your friendship but I'm just not ready to get serious with anyone right now. Anyone! Please, Ted, let me go. Please!"

I couldn't separate my rage from my fear. Marjorie said she had to get back to her apartment and study for an exam. I almost knocked my chair over as I pushed it back. I dropped her off at her apartment after which I returned the rented car to the airport and flew back to Palo Alto. It was a long and lonely flight.

Chapter Eighteen

Skiing in Aspen

I dropped my classes and left school and returned to Seattle. I gave up my desire for Chinese studies and even the possibility of government work. I decided to change my major to architecture because I had seen a movie in which an architect was the main actor. I was fascinated by the movie and that type of career, and I applied for the program at the UW but they didn't have any openings in the architecture program so I went into urban planning instead. I got a job as a busboy at the Seattle Yacht Club and I went to school.

I couldn't adjust to not having Marjorie in my life. I couldn't concentrate on my studies and I did poorly on tests. I left college during the first quarter of

1967 with several incompletes. I had to regroup and pull myself together.

I had always found solace in getting away. I had saved money from my busboy job and, in January of 1968, went on a trip to Lake Tahoe, Denver, Aspen, and Vale, where I skied until I got tired of it. Then I decided to go back East and visit my relatives.

So the breakup in your relationship with Marjorie was a major turning point in your life. Do you blame her for you becoming a serial killer?

That was a major turning point in my life but I don't blame her for the women I killed. You've got to understand, it wasn't Marjorie that was the problem. It could have been any of a hundred girls who might have come along at that time. The problem was that I had focused my entire life on the outcome of that relationship. Failure to me was completely unacceptable; I wouldn't allow myself to consider it as an option. I can't emphasize that point strongly enough. As I look back on it, I came on too strong. I smothered her. Also, she needed financial security and I was poor and often had to borrow her car or borrow money from her for gas.

Tell me about your first trip to Philadelphia.

A lot of it is a blur but there are some memories that stand out. I remember driving for hours and hours and, when I reached a destination, I skied until I was tired of it and then I'd drive again. The people I saw in the ski lodges and the restaurants and motels became players in my mind. When I saw a man who appeared to have status and wealth, I mentally demonstrated my superiority in a conversation with him. I'd look at beautiful girls and imagine that we were making love somewhere in the beautiful mountains that I had been driving through. I sat in booths at the back of restaurants where I could watch everyone without calling attention to myself. I spoke to them in my mind: "I'm watching you but you can't see me doing it. I'm invisible to you. I can sense who and what you are. I know your strengths and your weak parts. You can't harm me because you can't detect my presence. I will always be a mystery to you but, if I wanted to, I could always find you. You can never find me."

You were attempting to appease your depression with mental chess.

I had a very singular experience when I was at the ski lodge in Aspen. The weather was fantastic and the slopes could not have been more perfect. A very attractive blonde approached me as I was about to take my spot on the chair lift. I immediately pictured her breasts and her smooth shoulders. I mentally stroked the lines of her neck and I massaged her temples. For a moment, it was as if it was Marjorie again. I think it was a close repeat of the skiing trips Marjorie and I used to go on that called forth such a powerful image. I was disappointed when she took the chair in back of mine.

I played a mental game with her. We were at the top of a very high slope. She and two female companions started down the hill together. I followed them down and I swerved way out to the side and then sharply back, almost hitting one of them. I imagined that I separated her from her friends and was able to get her alone off in the pines. I didn't want to rape her. I wanted to steer her towards a cliff where we would both be killed but then I would cut to the side at the last moment. I sensed that I watched her go over the edge.

Then I was descending the hill in slow motion. I saw a number of large pines ahead of me and I had an urge to ski directly into them. I closed my eyes to better feel the vibration of my skis against the snow. The motion was fast and the wind against my face strong, and yet it was as if I was still moving very slowly. It was almost as if I could rise into the sky and ski above the trees. Somebody yelled for me to look out and I opened my eyes just in time to avoid hitting a huge pine. It was strange because I didn't experience the normal terror a person would have following a near-death experience such as this.

Chapter Nineteen

Two Elk

It was dark when I got to the dining room at the lodge to get something to eat. I got a sandwich and a bottle of beer and sat at a table beneath a group of magnificent animal mounts. They had a live dance band and, as I watched the couples circling the floor, my mind began spinning, like the slow movement at the edge of a whirlpool, inevitably revolving and then coming back to its point of origin. It reminded me of when Marjorie and I would waltz around the floor and then slide into our seats and laugh. I felt myself being pulled deeper and deeper into some dark vortex, a bottomless abyss somewhere far below me. I was awakened from it by a waitress asking if she could get me another beer.

I attempted to engage her in some small talk about the mounted animal heads on the walls around the room but she didn't respond. She had other tables to tend to. There was a head of a bobcat and a cougar on the east wall, three heads of buck deer on the north wall, and the head of a bull elk on the south wall. On the west wall there was a magnificent head of a large bull elk with a mounted cow elk next to it. The bull looked proud and even a bit arrogant. The cow elk had a softness about her. Each had black eyes that appeared alert and on guard. The cow elk was almost as proud as the bull. She was his, yet I knew he didn't control her. This was the most magnificent pair of animals I had ever seen.

I noticed an attractive girl sitting alone at a table drinking a beer. She was also studying the animals on the wall. I picked up my drink and went over and stood at the side of her table.

"Hi," I said, "I noticed you looking at those two magnificent creatures on that wall. My name is Ted Bundy. I'm from the Seattle area and I haven't seen such marvelous creatures up close. I've only seen them in books or in movies. They are elk, aren't they?"

She looked at me suspiciously for a few moments then answered, "They're local elk. They're scattered up and down this mountain range."

"You're from around here, then," I said.

"Well, I'm from Denver. I guess you could say I'm from around here."

I detected her uneasiness. She appeared to be in her twenties. She was still in her ski outfit, the color of which was faded as if it had been washed several times. Her lift ticket was still around her neck. Her gloves were stacked one on top of the other in the center of the table, turned sideways as if to signal to an unwanted guest that she didn't want company. Her eyes were sad but her gaze was steady and inviting. Mixed messages.

I continued, "I'm really fascinated by all these trophies. Did all of these animals come from around here?"

"Yeah," she said, "I think they did. John Beckham is the owner of this place. He can tell you about them if you're interested."

"Well," I said, "I'm intrigued by their beauty. I'd like to talk to him but I have to leave for Philadelphia early in the morning so I don't think I'll have a chance to do so. Do you hunt?"

She took a sip of her beer and nervously began playing with her napkin. "Yeah, I do some. I shot that buck up there," pointing to the north wall. "John is my uncle and he helped me shoot it and he had it stuffed."

I was playing her. Every question I asked called for an answer. Every comment I made demonstrated a sincere interest. I had learned previously that my broad smile and my eagerness to understand produced trust.

However, she was unaware that it was well practiced, contrived, calculated. This was the psychopath in you coming out. What did you ask her next?

You're probably right about that. I said to her, "I'm planning on coming through here again this spring. Is there someone who could take me up into the mountains where I could take some pictures of animals such as these? In their natural habitat?"

She said, "How did you happen to come here?"

"I'm a college student at the University of Washington," I said. "I'm working on a degree in art. I paint landscapes with animals like these in them. I plan on setting up an art studio when I finish my degree. I'm on my way to Philadelphia to see my grandparents. I stopped here to do some skiing and also to see if there was a possibility of setting up a studio here in Aspen."

Ted, why did you lie to her? Why couldn't you have simply informed her that you were a college student going into politics and that you were taking a brief break to visit relatives in the East?

An impressive lie that incites interest is better than boring truth. The purpose of the conversation was to establish a connection with the girl. You understand. You called it mind chess.

That term seems to bother you.

It makes me sound like someone with only evil intent.

But at this point you were developing fairly strong psychopathic characteristics and this mind chess game was part of the process. Tell me, did it work with that girl?

Yes. She softened and invited me to sit down. Her name was Ginger, so named after Ginger Rogers, her mother's favorite actress. The lodge was serving hot bread with honey so I ordered a round of bread and beer for both of us. We talked for a while. I became distracted by the elk mounts on the wall.

"You seem deep in thought," she said.

"That bull elk is so proud . . . so proud. I'll bet that cow was always running off with other bull elk. It's a shame that the only way he can hold on to her is for her to be dead. She is by his side now and she will never leave. She belongs to him. It will be that way forever. He will never need to be lonely again. Life is beautiful . . . but I guess death can also be beautiful."

I looked back at Ginger and I detected a frightened look in her eyes. She said it was time for her to retire for the evening and she excused herself and left. I continued staring at the two elk. They looked so alive. It wouldn't have shocked me had they jumped off the wall and run out the front door into the mountains. I pictured myself as the bull and since I found Ginger to be quite attractive, she was the cow. We were living deep back into the mountains where no one could bother us. It was a nice fantasy.

Once again you had escaped into a deep fantasy in the presence of a potential victim.

I didn't perceive her as a victim. She was my lover in my fantasy.

But, Ted, wasn't it that same way with the victims you killed?

You're twisting things again.

Am I? Wasn't every victim simply a prop in a fantasy production that all took place in your mind? After all, you bludgeoned all of your victims into unconsciousness before you had sex with them, and with some of them you even engaged in necrophilia. You severed the heads of some of your victims which you took with you in order to be able to continue with the fantasy after there was no whole person to interact with.

> Well, there may be some truth to that but you are exaggerating it out of proportion.

Let's go back to the ski resort. What did you do when you came out of the fantasy?

> I retired for the night and I left for Philadelphia the next morning. I drove straight to my grandfather's house. It was good to see them. They were a stable part of my life. When I was a child our family would go back to Philadelphia once every three or four years. I also visited with my aunt. I told them I needed a break from college and that I was staying only a couple of weeks after which I would visit my uncle Jack in Arkansas. I told them I wanted to take a trip to Manhattan Island to see the Statue of Liberty and other sites up in that area, particularly Vermont. They seemed hesitant. I don't think they were aware that I knew my mother had been in a home in Vermont for unwed mothers. Nevertheless, after a few days with them, they wished me the best as they sent me on my way.

> My plan was to find the place where I was born, but I dreaded what I might find.

Chapter Twenty

Elizabeth Lund Home for Unwed Mothers

I wanted to find the Elizabeth Lund Home for Un-
wed Mothers at Burlington, Vermont. I was born on
November 24, 1946, right around Thanksgiving. I
reached Burlington late in the afternoon. I rented
a room in a motel and drove around that night in
an attempt to find it. The home for unwed mothers didn't exist as such but the building was still
there. It was austere, appearing empty and cold. I
could picture my mother on the walk leading to the
door with a small suitcase in her hand, frightened
at having to be so far from home. I was angry at
my grandparents for making her go through this.
I thought about the cruel manner in which I first

learned that I was illegitimate. I was only thirteen years old at the time.

I don't know the exact date of Thanksgiving in 1946 when my mother was there but I imagine that it was somewhere around the 24th, which is my birthday. "Happy Thanksgiving mother," I thought, "You have just given birth to a baby boy that you didn't ask for and probably didn't want. It was such a severe sin that you had to be put away until this child was born because it would be too humiliating for people to know that this baby was a bastard child. Who is the father? Why couldn't you have told me who my father was? Why did I have to learn from my cousin that I was illegitimate? Every child has the right to have a father and a mother. Why in hell didn't you tell me?"

I vented my anger against my mother and then my father. I was also angry at my grandparents because they wouldn't allow my mother to have me in a normal hospital surrounded by a loving family. I was something to be ashamed of and it was evident that they were never going to tell me about all of this. It was obvious to me that I was tolerated but never loved.

The next day I obtained my birth certificate through civil registration. I knew what I would find, but I did it anyway. It didn't have the name of my father. I knew that his name wouldn't be there but it still devastated me nonetheless, just as it did when I was a child.

Chapter Twenty-One

34th Street

What did you do then?

I headed back towards Philadelphia the following morning but I decided to stop off in New York City to check out 34th Street. I had heard that this was a popular area for hard-core pornography. I had told my grandparents that I would likely spend several days in Vermont so they weren't expecting me back real soon. I drove into the heart of New York and found a parking space and a room at a relatively cheap hotel on one of the side streets near Times Square. I unpacked my suitcase, hung my clothes on hangers, laid out my shaving gear on a small shelf next to the bathroom sink, and walked to the

Square. The sun was at the horizon and the street lights were coming on.

I started down 34th street and I came to a large neon sign that spread across the front of a building: "Girls Girls Girls." Above the sign was the name of a restaurant. It was an older pre-war, red brick building with darkened windows. The man in the ticket booth had on a red shirt with a blue bow tie, and a striped jacket with wide lapels, and he reminded me of a circus barker. I was curious so I purchased a ticket and went in.

I went down a dark hallway and came to a large darkened room with flashing lights. Cigarette and cigar smoke hovered in the air. The odor of beer and whiskey was strong. The wooden table tops were prematurely old by the tearing at the surface with wire cleaning brushes. Greasy dirt was embedded in the deeper grooves. The black and white checkered linoleum on the floor had long lost its sharp pattern from myriads of shoes abrasively scraping against it. This could only be called a restaurant by the very drunk, the discarded street people left over from the war, the self-indulgent, or the self-deceived.

I was about to leave when three girls came out on the stage. I positioned myself at a table at the back corner of the room and, as I looked around, I saw some men who looked like college students. Some of the patrons appeared to be businessmen, possibly seeking something more exciting than what they had to look forward to at home. There was a guy up in front who looked like a loner, a guy who seemed terrified to ask a girl out for a date. He must have come here fairly often because the girls would wave to him periodically. One of the girls came down from the stage, danced around him, and brushed her breasts against the back of his neck. He handed her some money and she tucked it in her bra and went back up on stage. Everyone seemed to get what they came for. The business-men got a fresh array of images to fantasize about when they made love to their wives. The girls got a small salary for a few hours of work along with money inserted into their bra or their shorts if they gyrated enough. The owner of the restaurant got enough money to carry him through to the next month.

I had never been in a place like this. I had seen na-ked women in magazines but never had I watched a woman actually take off her clothes in this man-ner. These were beautiful young girls who were showing their bare breasts and they were moving in such a way as if they were inviting me to come up and touch them. The music was sometimes rapid, sometimes slow, but always hypnotic.

What effect did it have on you?

I was embarrassed being there but that feeling didn't last long. These other people were after the same thing I was after. I didn't have to peek through a window to see this. The young guys who looked like college students, like me, made me feel that I wasn't so abnormal. I stayed to the end of the show and then I went back to my hotel room with a new level of excitement. I felt I had advanced to a higher level of adventure. I got undressed, laid down on my bed, and I relieved myself in a deep fantasy about one of the girls I had seen that night.

I was still too aroused to be able to sleep so I watched TV for a while. They were playing a late-night rerun of a movie about the war. It piqued my interest for a few minutes as I watched recently returned soldiers in a ticker-tape parade march down the streets of New York. I wondered if my father had marched in a similar parade in Philadelphia. Had my father been a hero in the war? Had he done something glorious for his country? Had my mother been swept off her feet by his uniform and by the excitement over the war having ended? Was it only a one-night affair or had she known him before the war? Did she ever tell him she was pregnant with his baby? I felt deep sadness for my mother as I again pictured her walking up that cold cement walkway towards the front door of the home for un-wed mothers.

I was finally able to get to sleep. I decided to stay one more day. I explored all the adult book shops that I could find. I purchased a number of true crime magazines with pictures of nude bodies on the covers. I then went to the medical sections of the university libraries in the area in search of autopsy textbooks to enable me to learn as much as I could about the female body. I made photocopies of the parts that interested me and I returned to my hotel room to take it all in.

That night I went back to the dive I was at the night before. I saw the faces of some who had been there previously. The street guy was still sitting as close to the stage as he could get. It was as though he had never left. Had he been allowed to sleep in that spot?

The early show was a repeat of what I had seen the night before. After watching that show I went to a second bar and a third dive to see what they had to offer. Each successive place generated additional excitement over the one before. I returned to the first one for the late show. The attractive blonde was still there. She kept looking towards me as if she was curious about who I was. I entered into a fantasy in which I took her to an expensive restaurant and then back to an fancy hotel room where I gently caressed her body and then made love to her. It was exciting and she loved it.

So this was primarily a love fantasy.

Yes, at first. But then something very strange began to take place. The picture in my mind changed. It was not my decision for the picture to change but now it was as though I was watching it happen. I momentarily wondered how another part of my brain could take over my volitional control.

Someone seemed to have scrapped the old movie and had put a new one on in its place. It was me who was watching the first one but it was as if somebody else was watching this new one. It was this other person's private film yet he was allowing me to watch it. I couldn't figure out what it was he wanted me to see. This was very fascinating to me. I didn't want it to stop because I wanted to see what would happen next.

Tell me about this new movie in your head.

I was no longer in the restaurant with this beautiful blonde. We were back in this room, this dive, where I had come to watch her dance. It was empty except for the two of us. She was dancing on stage and she kept looking down at the table where the loner had been sitting but he wasn't there. I approached her to put money in her bra. She pushed me away without even looking at me. It incensed me that she would take money from a pathetic street tramp who had been sitting here but she wouldn't take money from me. She continued circling around the pole, always looking out as if she was trying to see somebody. Each time she passed me she looked right through me, as if I was invisible to her. I reached up and pulled her down on the floor and jerked off her skimpy clothes. I could feel a powerful energy rapidly rising from some deeper level within my body. I immediately recognized it as the evil side of me, this thing that was disrupting my life far more frequently than what I willed it to do so. It was powerful but was this his movie or was it mine?

I feared this side of me, yet I admired his cunning and his energy. He was pure power, devoid of conscience. He operated under his own rules. I had always maintained control over him but alcohol lowered my resistance and when I drank he appeared. It fascinated me because I sensed that he was my protector. He came to my aid when I was angry or sexually aroused. I hated him and I feared him, yet I also loved him. I could have made him turn off his movie and put mine back on but I didn't want to. I wanted to see what would happen next.

Someone yelled and I snapped back to reality. I was again sitting at the table with all the other people in the room and we were all watching the blonde dancer. I had spaced out again. It disturbed me, not so much that I had dissociated into a fantasy about taking this girl out to dinner, but that another part of me had taken over and had changed my imagery into his own fantasy. This thing had been within me for several years but now I wasn't sure if I was controlling him or if he was controlling me. It was as if he was beginning to create himself. He was taking on a life of his own and I feared the possibility of him having too much control. Still, I believed I could resist him when I wanted to but I didn't want to stop him right now because it was giving me an escape from my depression. He had a level of excitement and strength that I had never experienced.

The show ended and I stood up to leave. I was dizzy and I almost fell over. The next morning I couldn't remember having left the bar and having walked back to my hotel. I couldn't stop thinking about what had happened. I was very uneasy about entering into another deep fantasy like the one I had been in the night before but I wasn't sure I could stop it from happening again. I packed my things and I drove back to Philadelphia, then to Arkansas to visit my Uncle Jack, and then back to Tacoma.

Chapter Twenty-Two

Art Fletcher Campaign and Temple University

I felt a need to reestablish myself so I became a busboy in a Hilton Hotel and worked in a Safeway store at night where I stocked shelves, but I had to give up the busboy job because it was too many hours. I met a friend who was in the political arena and he encouraged me to work in the Art Fletcher campaign. I got involved with an influential group and I became chairman of a youth group in Seattle. I also worked for the New Majority for Rockefeller for President campaign, even though I wasn't yet 21, and had to sneak into taverns to drink with my colleagues. I saw Marjorie a few times but I didn't get any encouragement that we could get back together again. I felt I was in the process of rebuilding my life and she was about to graduate from college and to take a job in a stockbroker's firm. I still didn't have anything to offer her.

How did you like working in the campaigns?

Once again, I had found my purpose in life. It was exciting.

Being part of Fletcher's political campaign gave me stability and purpose. I was over some of my shyness. I still wasn't dating but that was all right. My social life centered around the elections. I went on campaign trips and could debate with the best of them. I was a personal driver for Art and his wife. I critiqued his speeches and I was a personal counselor to him. I enjoyed the drinking parties as well. I fit in.

I had curtailed my porn and my night junkets and I felt for the first time that this was the lifestyle that worked best for me.

What was Art's campaign like?

He was a positive person, a hard worker. When it appeared in the polls that he was falling behind, he'd remind us that it wasn't over until it was over. I asked him how he could remain positive in light of the evidence. "Ted," he said, "don't ever give up. You are defeated only when you believe you are."

I got into the dirty tricks arena when we went on campaign trips. On one occasion when I was at a party I was picked up by a woman and was taken to her place for the night, seemingly as a place to

> stay while away from headquarters. She was sepa-
> rated from her husband at the time. She was an
> hysterical person. I was drunk. During the night this
> woman came to my room and climbed in bed with
> me. That was my first sexual experience. Can you
> believe it, my first sexual intercourse was when I
> was drunk and a woman I hardly even knew was
> taking advantage of me?

You had indicated to me, and Marjorie had confirmed it, that you and Marjorie would lay naked together but you wouldn't have sexual intercourse.

> No, she said she wasn't ready for it yet.

It must have been very disappointing to you after years of experiencing passionate love-making in fantasy to have your first sexual intercourse in such a horrible manner as this.

> Well, I was drunk so I didn't experience it. It was
> something that happened to me rather than some-
> thing I wanted.

Art Fletcher lost the election, right? I imagine that was depressing for you.

> Very much so. Everyone was in the large hall watch-
> ing the election returns. As the night wore on, it was
> clear that he would lose. I had left to get a cold
> beer from the refrigerator when I heard the cheer-
> ing and I knew Art had come into the hall to give
> his farewell speech. It was depressing to hear him
> admit defeat. I went back to my apartment, turned
> Wagner up really loud, and got drunk. I fell asleep
> watching some late night movie.

> I went back to Seattle and got a job at a shoe store.
> I wanted to go back to college and eventually get

my law degree, but I wasn't ready for the U of W because I wasn't over Marjorie and there were too many memories associated with that campus.

Still, I needed to finish college in order to do anything more than to be a campaign worker or work in shoe stores or grocery stores. I decided on Temple University in Philadelphia because I had heard a person could get a law degree without first having a Bachelor's degree. I was able to live with my aunt which allowed me to keep my expenses at a minimum.

You started there in January of 1969 as I remember. Were you able to adapt to the college?

No. Temple University was located in an area that had a lot of crime and gang violence. The new buildings had no windows. There was a guard by some of the doors, and playgrounds had barbed wire around them. My goal was to study the nature of student populations to find some way to get the community involved in change.

What happened?

I couldn't pull myself together to do the work. I skipped lectures, guessed on tests, and attended class just often enough to pass the courses.

I was depressed and I became even more obsessed with stalking, which I would often do in the evenings. It was a strong power trip and I learned to do it in a manner so the girl wouldn't suspect that I was following her.

How would you do it?

Sometimes I'd walk behind the girl for a short distance and then I'd turn off in another direction. I had a sense about how long I could do this before she would become suspicious. Then I'd circle around and watch her. Sometimes I'd follow the girl by walking in front of her. I'd make a guess about which way she was likely to turn and I'd turn that way. She had no idea that I was stalking her because she was walking behind me. In this way I was able to follow girls from one side of the campus to the opposite side. I could follow a woman for several blocks in town without her having any awareness that I was there. I would fantasize about grabbing her and pulling her into an isolated dark area and raping her. I was constantly aware of where I was at the moment relative to my surroundings and the opportunities available for the rape.

Ted, you thrived on living a secret life, didn't you?

My night life and my fantasy world were the only things real to me. I had no career, no girlfriend, and no friends. I had no direction and I soon realized that I had made a mistake by coming to Temple University, but I couldn't leave. I'd have to stick it out for at least one semester and that's what I did. My fantasy life was my escape. Marjorie had left a black hole in me and I couldn't climb out of it.

Chapter Twenty-Three

Breakdown of a Personality

Ted, we've talked about the gradual deterioration in your emotional controls. You had come to realize that you were dissociating during a fantasy and it was beginning to bother you. You knew that pornography and fantasy were destructive and obsessive and yet you continued giving in to them. Smoking is a very difficult addiction to cure and yet people are able to do it. Why couldn't you stop the fantasy addiction?

> Smoking affects your physical health. When you do it everyone around you sees you doing it. There's no imagery with smoking. You don't daydream about smoking. There's a sedative effect but there's no feeling of power.

Many people believe that your problem was an addiction to pornography.

There's a lot of truth in that but, if that's all there was to it, I could have been able to masturbate to a picture of a couple having intercourse in various positions and that would have satisfied me. With most guys, that would have been enough because they have secure relationships in their lives that keep them at that level of involvement. Sex was not the primary motivation for my interest in pornography. In my case, the pornography was only a reminder of what I didn't have and a promise that it was out there waiting for me. All I had to do was to find a way to obtain it.

I had several talks with a serial rapist a few years back. He said that rape and sexual intercourse with a partner were two different needs. He reported a happy marriage and satisfying sex with his wife. Yet, he would still have to masturbate to thoughts about raping a woman, often on the same night after having engaged in an enjoyable sexual experience with his wife. As to why he had to rape, he said that while having intercourse with his wife he would fantasize about attacking a woman. It was so exciting to him that, following sex with her, he told his wife he was going out for a while. On several occasions he located a victim.

For you, was the dominance and control of the victim the important part of it?

Yes, that was part of it, but there was more to it than that.

What more were you after?

As strange as it sounds, I wanted companionship.

That's interesting. Dennis Nilsen of London killed 16 young men in his apartment. He said that in addition to the excitement, he was after the companionship. Let me read to you what he said, as reported by Masters in 1985:

> It was intense and all consuming . . . I needed to do what I did at that time. I had no control over it then. It was a powder keg waiting for a match. I was the match . . . The kill was only part of the whole. The whole experience which thrilled me intensely was the drink, the chase, the social seduction, the getting the "friend" back [meaning the essence of the "friend" would still be there], the decision to kill, the body and its disposal.
>
> The pressure needed release. I took release through spirits and music. On that high I had a loss of morality and danger feeling . . . if the conditions were right, I would completely follow through to the death . . . I wished I could stop but I could not. I had no other thrill or happiness.[33]

Jeffrey Dahmer had the heads of some of his victims in his refrigerator. John Wayne Gacy buried his victims in the crawl space under his house. He had a construction company and he could easily have buried his victims in a location where their bodies would never have been found. Why didn't he? It wasn't because he was too lazy to do so. He wasn't too lazy to go to work and earn a living. He wasn't too lazy to put on a clown suit and entertain kids in the local hospital. He wasn't too lazy to clear the streets in his area in Chicago from snow in the winters for his neighbors. Is it possible that he put the bodies of those kids there so he could have some form of companionship?

Come on Ted. That's crazy. What kind of companionship can a killer get from dead bodies in a crawl space under his house?

Why do you think serial killers take souvenirs from their victims?

To allow them to better relive the crime.

That's simplistic. Do you believe that's the only reason?

What other reason would there be?

I read that book on Nilsen as well. I remember Nilsen saying he wanted a friend and that after killing his victim the essence—or the spirit if you like—of his victim seemed to remain in his apartment?

But to most people that simply means that he was insane.

But was he found to be legally insane? Did he know right from wrong? Did he know his acts were against the law when he committed the crimes?

The courts found him to be legally sane, knowing right from wrong at the time of the crime.

Next you will say that he committed these crimes because he was a psychopath.

Is that not a possibility?

Of course it is. However, no one has been able to figure out just how a psychopath becomes one. The term "psychopath" is a description of behavioral traits. It's a descriptive, not an explanatory term.

At the point in your life when you went to Temple University, you were showing mild psychopathic characteristics. A few years later you were showing a heavy array of psychopathic traits. What happened in your case?

There were many problems with what was taking place within me. One problem was that I didn't have the maturity of mind at that age to fully understand what I was doing. I didn't see anything wrong with it. I wasn't hurting anyone and except for peeking in windows; I wasn't breaking any laws. Another problem was that I never prepared myself for failure. I would never give in to failure and, when I did fail, I turned to my tried-and-true solution, my fantasy life. In the beginning it worked every time. If something in my life came in conflict with it, I always held on to the fantasy but I never gave up my future goal of involvement in politics. I knew the time would come when I'd achieve it. It also was a big part of my fantasy life.

I started having to make choices regarding the guilt I was experiencing but I chose my fantasy world over other aspects of life. When the family activities interfered with my pornography, I withdrew from the family. When the preacher talked about sin and God, it got in the way so I gave up church as well. When I felt guilt—and I did feel a lot of it in the beginning—I made the decision to keep doing what I was doing and I gradually desensitized to the guilt. You can always find a reason why you are right and others are wrong. You could switch sides and argue the opposite and still convince yourself that you are right if you wanted to.

I came to believe there are no truths, only expediency. My involvement in the political campaigns convinced me there are always two sides to an issue, and the party that wins the election is not always the party that is the best one for the people but the one which can win the debates through the most eloquent oratory.

Everything was going along well until Marjorie and I broke up. I wasn't prepared for that to happen. She was my driving force. She was the basket I had put all of my marbles into. She was the link to my career. She validated my career. It was as if my career goals and Marjorie were pieces of a puzzle, locked together in a tight fit. When you pull those pieces apart the picture is completely destroyed. When a person is as lonely as I was and this person finds a partner who accepts him, as Marjorie seemed to do with me, it validates every dream he has about his future. My fantasy world had only one purpose up to that time. In every fantasy I had, there was a beautiful girl that I could devote my life and career to, one who admired me because of my greatness and, in all humility, I could show her how much I loved her. I had put this imaginary girl up on a pedestal and over and over, thousands of times; I worshiped her. There was absolutely no thought about the possibility of finding another partner should this one end. When it did end it was as if every coordinated and consistent thought about my future had been violently torn apart from every other similar thought. Nothing connected with anything. Every time a thought came, it was like a fragmented sentence which broke into small pieces before it could be spoken. It was if a strong electric voltage had been sent through my brain severing every neuron from every other neuron. The only thing that remained was this insatiable urge to call Marjorie and beg for forgiveness and plead for her to take me back. I wanted to tell her I would change in any way she wanted me to, but of course I couldn't. But even that was a fragmented mystery because I didn't know what I had done wrong. I was left with the feeling of that teenage boy with acne that nobody wanted around.

I tried to keep moving but I couldn't detect a viable direction so I was going nowhere. I was like a sailing ship against an oncoming wind. You tack back and forth in an attempt to make some headway but at the end of the day you find that you are in the same position that you were in that morning.

I was able to curtail my fantasy life when things were going well with Marjorie but when we broke up I turned to those images as often as chance would provide. I would eliminate all distractions around me so I could actually be in the presence of the woman in my mind. Sometimes it would be Marjorie but at other times it would be somebody I had seen that day. When I was able to create the full setting in my mind, including the conversation, the clothes she was wearing, and sometimes the smell of her perfume, it was by dissociating from everything around me. I was there. I was living it. I could hear every nuance of change in her voice pattern. I could see the terror in her eyes when she realized that I was going to take what she wasn't willing to give to me. I had been knocked off my pedestal and this fantasy elevated me to the highest point on that platform once more.

You have to understand, the closer I got to the real thing, meaning raping a woman, the more excited I got about actually doing it. After a while, daydreaming about rescuing a beautiful woman from a disastrous death in the mountains had lost its power to excite me. I knew that sooner or later I would actually have to rape someone or it would lose all of its meaning. There was no beautiful woman to rescue but there were many women walking the streets every day who could be a target for rape.

I was gradually losing my powers of control against this powerfully evil process inside of me. I could see what could happen if I didn't stop him and it terrified me. However, I had convinced myself that when it was absolutely necessary to do so, I could stop him.

Why didn't you get into therapy or get on medications for depression?

I didn't believe in them. Those devices were for weak and emotionally sick people who needed someone to tell them what was wrong with them and how they should live their lives. I didn't think of myself as a child or as crazy. I needed no one to tell me what was wrong with me.

Chapter Twenty-Four

Spring 1969

So what happened when you went back to Philadelphia?

> The classes were boring. I couldn't force myself to study. On weekends I went to New York and frequented some of the same bars I had gone to the year before. Honestly, Al, it was as though I was just there. I hadn't realized it had made such an indelible impression on my mind.

But the previous year you left New York to get away from it. You dissociated while you were in a fantasy and it frightened you. Why would you take a chance on tempting the Fates?

> I was less afraid of it now.

What do you mean?

I had relived that experience in my mind so many times since then that I felt I was in control. I could pull myself out of a fantasy at will.

So, did you practice extracting yourself from a deep fantasy?

Well, I did a few times but once I decided I could, I didn't try any longer.

Why not?

It was too painful to not complete a fantasy. When you stop halfway through a deep and intense imagery process such as that, it's like setting a plate of food in front of a starving person and then jerking it away after he has had only a few bites of it. You feel even more anxious and depressed than before you started the fantasy. A deep fulfilling fantasy isn't the same as a daydream. It's a lengthy and a very profound process initiated by a triggering mechanism. Once it has been set into motion you can't end it until it has run its course. It's hard to explain. The only thing I can liken it to is when you are completely involved in a movie or a sports event and someone calls you away from it. If you multiply that feeling of having to stop by ten then you will get some idea of what I am talking about.

What role does stalking play in it?

Stalking is a major part of it because again it's an active behavior rather than sitting at home masturbating to a picture. However, I believe there are a couple types of stalking.

How do you mean?

I have talked with some stalkers in here. There's the type who builds a complete fantasy life around one person. This person may be someone he has never met, like an actress. The dangerous aspect of this type of stalker is that even though he has never actually met his victim, in his fantasy he has taken her to dinner, bought her gifts, engaged in lengthy conversations, discussed marriage, and he has helped her out hundreds of times when she was in need. He has given himself to his victim and, in his mind, he has established a strong bond of trust with her. This type of stalker sees himself as her keeper, her confidant, her trusted friend, and her lover. He will do anything for her and in return he feels that she is obligated to him. If he sees her with another man he is enraged because he feels she has betrayed him and needs to be punished.

The other type is the person who goes out looking for a victim, any victim. This is sometimes called trolling. With a serial killer, any and all women are potential victims. That is the way it was with me. I would spend hours trolling for a victim. Once I saw a woman get out of her car and go into a bar. I let the air out of one of her tires and waited for her to come out. I was planning to offer her my help and then attack her. However, before I could get to her, she went back into the bar and a couple of guys came out and changed her tire.

Were you frustrated by the loss of your victim?

Well of course. I had waited over two hours for her to come out of the bar and see her flat tire. She turned and walked back into the bar before I could get to her. It was very frustrating.

Chapter Twenty-Five

The First Attack

So, what happened in 1969? Why did you stay at Temple only the one semester?

> I stayed only one semester because it was boring and I couldn't settle down to the class requirements. The fantasy and stalking wasn't giving me what I wanted. The more I enjoyed the fantasy of forcing myself on a woman, the more I wanted the real thing. The urge became so strong I couldn't sleep. I kept going out at night looking for victims. When I saw an attractive woman I pretended how I would attack her. I stood in the shadows in a park just off campus and went through this pretend game with several women who walked by me. I could see them without them seeing me, which

was a real trip. This one was too fat. That one too old. That one too young. The next one too ugly. But the next one . . . ah, she . . . she . . .

You're doing it again aren't you? Fantasizing?

I was remembering one night when I was on campus watching girls walk from one building to another. A beautiful girl came towards me and I felt I *had* to follow her. I didn't have any particular plan at that point; I just felt that I had to follow her. It was a need more than just a desire, and if I didn't find a way to satisfy that need I knew I would feel horribly anxious and depressed.

She walked past several buildings and then took an exit path, leaving by way of the north side of the campus, and headed up 13th street. I stayed far enough behind her. She didn't look back. She went into an apartment complex. There are a lot of trees along the street and I was able to easily position myself across the street in the front entrance of a building where I could watch from the cover of a tree. I remained there for about an hour wondering which apartment she went into. I tried to detect a light coming on in one of the windows shortly after she went in the front entrance. When a light didn't come on I decided that she likely had an apartment towards the back of the building. I went home but determined that I would come back the next night.

I couldn't sleep that night. I was too excited to concentrate in any of my classes the next day so I walked to her apartment two or three times to completely familiarize myself with the area and with the movement of the traffic and people. The traffic was fairly heavy during the day but it dropped off sharply after 6:30 pm. The same with people on the street. As evening approached, I was waiting in my spot across the street. About 8:30 in the evening she came down the street from the direction of the campus and into her apartment building. Again, there was no light that came on in the front set of apartments. Very few people walked that street after dark and there was only two who passed that second night. One was an old lady carrying some groceries from a small store up the street and another was a drunk.

There was a narrow path between her building and the next building down. I estimated where I would have to position myself in order to intersect her path when she was at the front door of her building. I would terrify her by catching her off guard. She would likely be in deep thought and I could have my hand over her mouth as I pulled her back and down a ways into the alleyway. That's where I would rape her and I'd exit out the other end of the alley.

It sounds like you're reliving it now.

Ah, well, yes, frankly.

Did you rape her that night?

No. It was two nights later that I almost had my chance. I disguised myself to some degree in case she was a student from the university. Everything worked well until I grabbed her and started pulling her towards the alley. I hadn't planned on a woman fighting so violently. She scratched at my face and bit my hand and when I yelled and let go she kicked me and slapped my face. She continued fighting me and I pushed her away and ran down the alley. I walked for several blocks and then back to my car which was parked on the other side of campus. I took to the dark streets because I didn't want anyone to see the blood on my face.

I couldn't believe I had done that. I cried and I promised myself I would never do it again. I felt very guilty and I was terrified of getting arrested and locked up in jail. I thought of Marjorie and of what she would think of me if she knew what I had done. For the next several weeks I attended to my studies and stayed at home.

Did you go back to that apartment again?

No, I was afraid that if she saw me she might recognize me. I went to my classes and came home. I checked the paper and found a small article about it around page three but it didn't say much.

Were you aware that you were approaching the time when you wouldn't be able to stop yourself and that you would commit a rape?

I was fearful that it could happen, yes. However, I reasoned that it was like a person who had always had a deep desire to visit Paris. He reads everything he can about it, he buys records of their music, he watches movies filmed on location there, and finally he saves up the necessary money and goes there. After he has finally vacationed for a week or two, he has satisfied his urge and he can return home and go on to other things in his life. In my case, I felt that once I had engaged in one rape, it would satisfy my need and curiosity and I would finally get it out of my system. Most people who climb Mt. Everest following years of wishing don't go back and do it again. That was my reasoning.

But it didn't work that way with you, did it?

Well, no, but I thought it would.

Chapter Twenty-Six

The First Homicides

Ted, the first attempted homicide attributed to you was on January 4, 1974. However, you indicated your first attack on a victim was that woman in the late spring of 1969. I can't believe that you didn't attack anyone from then until January of 1974. That would be almost five years.

Why do you think that?

Because the attack on the woman in Philadelphia was a clumsy attempt often seen in an unskilled rapist. The attack on the girl in 1974 was skillfully planned and executed. The killer had honed his skills to a sadistic art, much like the banker in that book who had sex slaves in his basement.

But the one in 1974 was not a homicide. She lived.

She only lived because the person committing the crime didn't check to see if she was dead before he left her apartment. It's obvious the intent was to kill her. The crime suggested confidence, patience, and dedicated stalking. The Ted who attacked the woman in Philadelphia is a far cry from the Ted who attacked that college freshman in her apartment on January 4th, 1974.

From the summer of 1969 to the end of 1973 you had evolved from a person attempting to make a fantasy come alive to a purposeful killer. You said that after the attempted rape in Philadelphia you became depressed and you swore to yourself that you would never do it again. Yet you did and far worse. Ted, that college student in January of '74 was not your first homicide victim. Your clear intent *was* to kill her. You had killed, or at least attempted to kill, prior to '74. Who was your first victim?

> But how do you know there was another victim between those two events?

Because Richard Larsen, the associate editor of the Seattle Times, who wrote *BUNDY: The Deliberate Stranger,* wrote an article in the Seattle Times paper about it. You reportedly told a psychologist by the name of Dr. Art Normal, who was working on an assessment on you for the court in Florida, that you had killed two girls in the summer of 1969, and this information was conveyed to Dick Larsen.

> Well, all right. I guess there's no sense in keeping it to myself. After my attempting to rape that girl in Philadelphia, I promised myself that I would never again attack another girl. I held to that until that summer. I had completed school and could see that it wouldn't work out for me to stay another semester. I wasn't doing well there and I didn't fit

in with any group. I didn't have any money and I missed Seattle. I wanted to go back home to continue my education.

I decided to take one more jaunt to New York City. After a day there I crossed over to New Jersey and I spent the day on the beach. It was a warm day and I was turned on by the girls in very skimpy bathing suits. I got up a conversation with two very attractive girls sunbathing on the beach. I was friendly and, since there were two of them, I believe that each felt safe with her friend there. Had there been only one girl I'm sure it would have been different.

It was a beautiful day and I felt very amorous. The girls had hitchhiked there and I offered to give them a ride. I said I had a car that I was delivering back to San Francisco.

So what happened?

It was very strange. As we were riding along the freeway, I had an intense urge to rip the one girl's clothes off. When we left the beach, they had put their street clothes over their bathing suits and that really upset me. I don't remember ever having been that close to two almost-naked bodies. Something began nagging at me to take the opportunity. But you need to understand it wasn't a formulated plan to do anything specific. I just wanted to touch them. As we drove away from the beach, I felt the opportunity slipping from me. I remember fighting within myself. Part of me had wanted to attack and rape them back on the beach but the logical side of me knew that it was an extremely bad idea. When we left the beach I thought the urge would go away. But it didn't. I think it's something like a person addicted to cigarettes who turns down one and then feels a deep regret that he did. I was so close to those naked bodies. So close. I couldn't let go of that feeling.

I attempted to keep control over myself by talking about their careers and my career and anything else I could come up with to distract me from this powerful urge. It was as if some part of my mind knew what was going to happen and it was trying to stop me.

It's very hard to describe to you. All of the energy in my body seemed to flow into my brain and I was becoming confused. We were out in the country when rage exploded within me.

I grabbed the one girl by the neck and I turned off on a side road. The other girl started screaming. I could see the terror in their eyes but it was too late to stop. I had passed the point of no return. We pulled off in a spot away from the road where we were alone. There were no houses around. I told them I didn't want to hurt them. The one girl started to cry and I grabbed her and choked her until she was unconscious. I was really confused. I didn't want to rape the other girl but I had come too far to stop. After I was done raping them, I killed both of them.

Why?

I couldn't allow them to report me to the police. But that wasn't all. I was in a rage over what I had just done and I hated them, as if it was their fault that they had been raped. If I ever had any hope that there was a God and that this God could forgive me, I knew it was out of the question for me now.

I knew everything in that instant. Except for the killing of those girls, I had lived this moment hundreds of times in my mind. Words to you now cannot but convey a tiny amount of what went through my mind as I looked down on those two girls. Ted Bundy, for all intents and purposes, was dead. I didn't think like him anymore.

Ted, we talked about the entity that you had been building up within you. Where was the entity when you killed those girls?

I was the Entity, or, more importantly, the Entity was me. I no longer struggled with the fear of hurting someone. The decision was made for me. At that moment everything I had believed about values and safety and consequences left me. It was as if I was watching the event happen, like someone else was doing it. "Wow, look at that," I thought. "Isn't that interesting? I've never seen anything like that before."

Could you have stopped it at that point?

No, not at all. For a moment before killing the first girl I heard something inside shouting to me not to do it but, when I struck out, there was an immediate suspension of all ethical beliefs or concerns about anything outside the realm of that moment.

It was like watching an exciting movie that I didn't want to end. I wanted to keep on watching to see what would happen next. But then it did end.

Go on.

It ended very suddenly and I was standing over by the bodies of those two girls. I remember a line from the Boston Strangler: "It wasn't like it was me; Mr. Ultimately—it was like it was someone else I was watching." I felt that same way.

Did you regret what you had done?

Oh yes, most definitely. Did I feel remorse? Absolutely. But it's not what you might be thinking.

What do you mean?

I had a deep revulsion over what I had done. I was horrified at the sight of it. Yet, I felt peace.

Peace? I don't understand.

That person standing, looking down at those two girls, was not me. It was not Ted Bundy. It was the same body, the same family, the same aspirations, but it wasn't the same person as the one who had been with those two girls on the beach a few hours before. That Ted Bundy had died when those two girls were killed. It was now a different Ted standing there.

You need to understand, it *was* me, I knew who I was but at that moment it was as if there were two of me. That other part, that other person, conceived through loneliness, fantasy, and masturbation, and nourished through practicing dissociation, that part was now more alive than ever before. There were several minutes following the deaths of the girls that *he* was still in control.

I couldn't understand why I felt peace. It took me several years to come to grips with that feeling. But still, as I look back on it, I don't know if it was him or me that was experiencing peace. It's still very strange to me how a person can kill someone and feel peace from it.

Did you ever figure it out?

I think so. I didn't remember attacking them but I knew I was the one who had done it. As I looked down on the bodies the terror I felt was not for them. It was for me. I knew what I did was wrong, completely wrong, but the accompanying feeling of guilt wasn't there. It was like I had done nothing of significance. I have often thought about that since then—the remorse factor. There wasn't any re- morse. Prior to the killing of those girls, when fear would come over me about the possibility of killing someone, I would tell myself: "Why? That would be something terrible to do. That's another person, another human being's life, and they have just as many rights to walk the face of the earth as I do." Now that I had killed them, that thought no longer had any significance for me.

Did you feel anything for those girls?

Yes, but if I felt sympathy for the girls it was masked by the interplay of more powerful emotions propelling me towards my ultimate goal of avoiding detection. But I did feel sad.

But no guilt?

> If you met two sisters at a party and you laughed and danced with them throughout the evening and you later learned that both had been killed in a violent accident, how would you feel?

I'd be very sad, of course.

> Would you feel guilt?

Well, no. I didn't kill those two sisters. In your case, however, you did kill them.

> That's what I'm trying to tell you. I knew logically that I had caused their deaths but, emotionally, it was not me. It was this other thing in me that took over and killed them. I think it's similar to a person who has serious anger issues. When he has a blackout and strikes out at someone, he doesn't remember having done so. Logically, he knows he did it but since he has no memory of it he feels bad but he doesn't experience the deeper feeling of guilt. He doesn't possess the awareness that he did it.

It sounds as if you are trying to excuse away your responsibility. Ted, almost no one believes in this so-called entity, or whatever you want to call it.

> I'm not saying I didn't do it. I'm aware that I killed those girls. However, I didn't *feel* that I had done it.

You said you felt sad. Tell me about that.

> I felt sad that their lives had ended. I was sad that they wouldn't have families and careers. I was sad

that I had lost an opportunity to get to know them better.

How did it change you?

The change that occurred within me was more profound than anything I could ever have imagined. I wanted to rip the memory out of my mind. I couldn't believe that I had just killed two young girls. I stared at them with disbelief. I was confused. I looked around to discern where I was at. Everything appeared different. It was warm but a breeze was blowing. It seemed incongruous that everything around me could appear so calm while the bodies of two girls lay at my feet. I wanted to feel terribly guilty but instead there was that unexpected feeling of peace.

Talk about that, will you?

It took years for me to understand it but I have finally been able to make sense of it. I had been struggling within myself over the urge to rape a girl. I pictured it in my mind hundreds of times and I really wanted to do it but I was afraid of getting caught and of what it would do to my career. The violent struggle was between the overwhelming urge with the anticipation of the experience and the fear from the anticipation of getting caught. When one gives in to an aggressive urge that one has been fighting against for years there is a feeling of calming peace, not because you experienced the violent act but because the struggle is now over. There is no longer the question of should you do it or should you not do it. It's done.

Are you talking about killing the girls?

> No. I'm talking about the fight that goes on within a person over anything he desperately wants to do yet knows he shouldn't do. I had no intention of killing anyone. I wanted to rape a girl but certainly not kill her. At first I blamed the girls. I shouted, "You did it to yourselves. You are to blame for your own deaths! If you hadn't worn those skimpy bathing suits this never would have happened!"

Did you really believe they brought it on?

> No, not really, but I wasn't ready to accept the fact that I had killed them. My mind couldn't grasp the full meaning of it all. It was an act I had convinced myself that I would never ever do and, now that I had done it, the immediate shock forced my mind to attempt to locate a cause other than within myself.

What other thoughts or feelings did you have at that moment?

> Homicide is a transformation. It changes a person in ways he can never completely understand. To some extent I felt like the devil but to some extent I felt like God.

God?

> Yes. I could permit life to remain or I could take it away. I had decreed that those girls should die and I carried out the sentence.

But surely being God is much more than simply giving life or allowing it to be taken away. God is love and forgiveness and strength. You were evil. You were vengeful and weak. You allowed this sinister thing within you to get out of control.

> But I couldn't see that I was doing anything wrong. I had the same goals and hero fantasies as any other boy my age.

Yes, but you changed those hero fantasies into revenge fantasies and you allowed yourself to dwell on them. You even taught yourself to dissociate into a fantasy so that it would seem to be more real to you. You created the phantom in you. The only life the shadow had was that which you gave it. It would not have come alive had you not willed it to do so.

> But all I wanted was to see what it would be like to attack a woman. I was able to keep my normal daily activities separate from this vicious side of me.

> I didn't know what to call this thing that I had created within myself. I could understand the Passion Play in Europe where an actor lives a part so intensely that he incorporates into his own personality the full range of attributes of that part and he continues to feel and act that part and, when the Passion Play is over, he has a difficult time changing back. I imagine at times he doesn't know which personality is his real one. It was that way with me.

Are you referring to the entity?

> Over the years its power increased until it seemed to take on a life of its own. It became easy to slip into that character, and entering into a fantasy was like acting out the part on a stage. But killing a woman was never part of my fantasy; I never let a fantasy go that far.

Chapter Twenty-Seven

Elizabeth Kendall

Ted, tell me about Elizabeth Kendall and the impact she had on you.

If it hadn't been for Liz, I don't know what would have become of me. I was very dejected when I got back to Seattle. I had no plans, no job, very little money, and only a vague idea of what I wanted to do. The only two places where I felt any comfort was on college campuses or working in political campaigns. No one was running for any major political office so that option wasn't available. I got a job and an apartment in the College District by the University of Washington. I still planned on going to college but I had to earn money first.

I couldn't get the images of those girls out of my mind. On one hand I deeply regretted their deaths but, on the other, I began wishing I had taken longer with them.

What do you mean?

It's that "opportunity lost" thing again. If I had known I was going to kill a woman then I should have made the most of it. It's like a starving person being put in front of a table of food. He gobbles it down so quickly, he doesn't enjoy it but later he wishes he had taken longer to enjoy it more. I didn't want to harm any more girls but the urge to do so kept coming back.

Why? One would think that you would feel so horrible about what you had done that you would avoid all thoughts of ever wanting to do it again. If you were able to avoid the guilt then why were you not able to avoid the killing fantasies as well?

Once you have felt enjoyment or peace after having killed someone, the act of killing is now part of who you are. With me, I didn't plan on killing again and I certainly didn't consider myself to be a serial killer. That self-image comes after the further homicides.

But if—and I'm only saying *if*—you were the one who killed that little girl when you were 15, then this would be your second incident.

If I had killed her, then maybe so. However, that one would not be the same because it was so completely accidental. In that one, there was no anger and no extreme level of lust. It was simply a case of a curious teenager who became scared. It's the second homicide that makes a person think that he might be a serial killer.

All right, but before talking about that one, let's talk about Liz. She was an important part of your life. Right?

Most definitely. She gave me more of a feeling of normalcy and of family than I had ever felt.

In her book, *The Phantom Prince*, she wrote that she met you in the Sandpiper Tavern on Halloween, 1969. What were you doing there?

I went there to get a beer and to dance. It was a tavern and dance hall. I danced with some of the girls there—most were college students—and I noticed this girl who kept glancing over at me from her table. I asked her to dance and she accepted after which we both danced with other partners. A little later she came over to my table and started up a conversation. It was obvious that she had been drinking, but then so had I. We were both somewhat drunk and maybe that's why it was so easy for us to get a conversation going. She told me she was divorced and had moved up to Seattle with her daughter at the encouragement of her friend.

In her book she said you told her that you had been living in Philadelphia, going to Temple University, and had come to Seattle to go to law school. You told her you were writing a book on Vietnam. You even spoke with a British-like accent and you wore clothes that were a cut above what the others were wearing. All of these things were lies. Why did you feel it was necessary to lie to her?

After having killed two girls, telling a few lies meant nothing. I didn't anticipate that I would ever see her again after that night. I lied to her because by then there was very little difference between the truth and a lie for me. It didn't matter to me what I said to her, or to any other woman. The important thing was the impression it made on them.

And what impression did it make on Liz?

She was smitten. It worked. We talked through the evening and then I drove Liz and her friends home in Liz's car. We stopped at the babysitter's to pick up her daughter. I didn't have a car at that time. By the time we got to her apartment she was too drunk to drive me home so she suggested I stay there for the night.

She was very embarrassed that she had brought home a man from a bar and she tried to ignore you for the next three days but you continued to maintain contact with her. You began to court her. You started making dinners for her and her daughter at her apartment. She was really impressed with your knowledge of wines and cooking. You read children's books to her daughter, Tina, and you watched cartoons with her on Saturday mornings. A little later you found a larger and cheaper apartment for the two of them because you felt that where she was living wasn't safe enough. She was convinced that you were the genuine thing. She fell in love with you very quickly and she referred to you as her prince. It's interesting to me that later, after you had been convicted of killing women and she learned how evil you really were, she was still willing to talk about all of the wonderful things she saw in you. She must have really loved you.

And I was really in love with her.

But how could you be in love with her—and with her family, I might add—and be so devious?

When we started going together our sexual engagements were very passionate. I wasn't as excited about the relationship as I was with Marjorie but I was much happier and more content. I had just killed two girls and my life was in shambles at that point. She provided stability.

But she made demands on you that you couldn't accept, didn't she? She began pressuring you about getting married.

Yes.

And even though sex with her was exciting and passionate, it didn't satisfy your lust for something more violent.

That's right.

So life with her, no matter how satisfying it was at times, was never enough.

No, it wasn't.

Is that what you meant when you said you had crossed a line by killing those girls?

Yes. When you get a taste for that form of violence, you always have a need for more.

When I was a kid, it was said that once a dog tasted blood when killing a chicken you couldn't stop him from killing other chickens. You either had to lock up the chickens so that he couldn't get to them or you had to lock up or kill your dog. Is that what it was like for you?

The only way you can stop a serial killer is to lock him up or kill him. A serial killer cannot stop killing. It just doesn't work that way.

Oh, come on Ted. Any other habit can be broken. If a man has been smoking for 30 years and a doctor tells him he will be dead in six months if he doesn't stop, he will usually stop. You said you felt sad for the girls. Why didn't that stop you? Your life was deteriorating rapidly but this didn't stop you. If you got caught, which was surely to happen, it would ruin your career and your reputation, let alone result in your execution, but the awareness of this didn't stop you from killing. Ted, there was nothing to gain and everything to lose by killing. Why did you continue doing it?

> I couldn't stop! God knows how many times I wanted to but I couldn't! I constantly did things with Liz and Tina in an attempt to have a normal family life. I went with her to Utah to meet her parents and relatives and I got along with them very well. I helped her mother in the kitchen fixing holiday meals and I loved doing it.

She wanted to get married and you agreed to it. You went with her to Salt Lake to inform her parents and everybody seemed happy with it. When you got back she took you to get a marriage license and then she began to make wedding plans and that made you angry. When I talked to you in Utah you said she didn't have the personality to be a politician's wife. Is that why you didn't want to marry her?

> She was shy and reserved and she wasn't comfortable around other people, especially important dignitaries. I enjoyed coming home to her and Tina and spending nights and weekends with them, but I wanted a woman like Marjorie. I wanted to be a father, not a stepfather. Liz was insecure and she was becoming an alcoholic.

Ted, was there anything to the fact of you being an illegitimate child that kept you from marrying her? She mentions in her book that you came over one night shaking and in tears because you were illegitimate and you thought that she wouldn't want to marry you because of it.

> That was a serious concern for me at the time. I was so angry at my mother because she never told me, and I had to learn it from my cousin.

How did you get out of the marriage agreement?

> I told her I needed to finish college and then get a job so that I could support her. That worked for a short while but she again started pushing for us to get married. She said that our sleeping together was a bad example for her daughter. We got into an argument and I tore up the marriage license.

Out of sheer anger or did you start the argument for an excuse to tear up the license?

> I set it up. She told me her parents were coming up for the weekend and she wanted to get married while they were there. She asked me to take my things out of her closet so her parents wouldn't know she and I had been sleeping together. I said she was childish and wasn't ready to get married and I tore the license in small pieces and walked off. She went home and started drinking.

But you couldn't stay away. You went back to her apartment and told her how much you loved her and you stayed with her that night. That was a perfect time for you to end the relationship but you couldn't do it. Why not?

> I couldn't stand being without her. I didn't want to get married right then but I couldn't give up the relationship.

Chapter Twenty-Eight

The Law School Fiasco

You had become quite the psychopath by this time. You stole items from stores and you seemingly felt no guilt about it. There's a story about you walking out of a store with an eight-foot Benjamins tree. You lowered it down through the roof of your Volkswagen in order to get it home. You stole tools and various other things as easily and as comfortably as another person who might pay for them. Even when Liz commented about it, you brushed her off. You had no desire to change your behavior.

> I had been engaged in theft for a few years including clothes, furnishings for my home, and tools. It simply didn't mean anything to me. I was very good at it.

You had been with Liz for six months and all during this time you held with your story that you had finished college and would be going to law school at the University of Puget Sound, starting winter semester. When you missed the start of the winter semester at UPS, you told Liz that your transcripts from Temple University hadn't come through on time. Liz was quite resourceful and she checked with UPS only to find that law school started with the fall semester. She realized that you had been lying to her all along. It was only then, six months into the relationship, that you finally told her that you still had two years of college before you could even think about law school. It seems that she was so dependent on you that even with this new information about your lies she couldn't leave you.

> She was very angry about it but she was willing to stay with me. If anything, it seemed to bring us closer together once that it was out in the open. She said she would put me through college and she did. I regained my focus for college and a career and this time I did very well in college.

But, Ted, why didn't you tell her the truth before that point? You knew that sooner or later it would all come out in the open. When she confronted you about it, you were calm and it didn't seem to bother you that she had discovered your lies. From what she said in her book, you didn't feel any guilt about having deceived her.

> No, I had conditioned myself to not feel any guilt. And I didn't. Also, I had succeeded in every criminal and evil thing I had ever done and I didn't anticipate that I would ever fail at doing so. As to why I didn't tell her about college, there was no need to do so before that time. When I was ready to start going to college again, I would tell her. It was nothing that she needed to worry about.

You have been talking about me as a psychopath, a person with no feelings. You need to understand something. I still had strong emotions, sometimes extremely strong. I would get angry. I would get depressed. I could still enjoy the emotional intimacy and companionship that comes with sex. I enjoyed spending time with Liz's family. I was able to feel most of the normal emotions.

I had only two primary problems that would fit your definition of a psychopath. These problems were in reference to the inability to feel guilt or feel compassion.

This was a serious problem because . . . ?

Because I *felt* the need for intimate contact with a woman but I was incapable of putting myself in the woman's position. I couldn't sense her needs. She, along with everyone else, had become objects. Beautiful objects but, still, objects. People had beauty, but so did animals, and I felt that if you believe that everything in nature were part of God's creations then one species was no more important than another. To kill a human is no different than killing an animal.

Interaction with others was like a game. I had areas of power, as did my opponent, and if I could outmaneuver him—or her—through my skill and patience, I did so. It's a magnificent art and skill that reflects superiority.

But don't think for a moment that I didn't have feelings for justice. I have always been in favor of helping the poor and those being discriminated against. I was a conservative Republican and I believed in honoring your beliefs. When some people think of a psychopath, they think it's a person who has no feelings, no loyalty, and a lack of ability to fight for a cause. I was a campaign aide for the Dan Evans reelection for governor campaign in 1972. I worked hard for him and I got to know him personally. I was deeply emotionally involved with that campaign.

Chapter Twenty-Nine

Return to School

In the summer of 1970 you started back to school at the University of Washington, majoring in psychology. You did well in school but you maintained a relationship with a convicted felon on parole who had a pawn shop. You smoked pot with him, right?

> Yes, at times. However, alcohol was my drug of choice. I never got involved with the heavier drugs like acid, heroin, or cocaine.

How was the relationship between Liz and you at this time?

> Everything was calm and peaceful again and it remained so until in the spring of 1971.

What happened then?

> Liz asked me one day how I would feel if she went on a date with some guy she worked with. It cut deep but what else could I say than to tell her she could do anything she wanted to do.

And you didn't suspect that she was doing this to make you jealous, to force the issue about you marrying her?

> I thought that marriage might be her motivation.

But?

> But there was nothing else I could do. I *couldn't* marry her. It was an absolute impossibility.

Why?

> Have you ever seen the film *Manhunter*?

Yes. That's the movie made from Thomas Harris's book, *Red Dragon*.

> The story is about a serial killer who is living alone in an isolated area away from the city. He kills entire families and tapes their eyelids open as if he wants them to admire him, even in death.

Yes, I remember that.

> The entire film is quite accurate but there are a few scenes which are extremely accurate. You remember the blind girl who befriended him?

Yes. She accepted him even though he was disfigured.

> He takes her to his place and he tells her he has some work he has to finish before he can spend time with her. She sits on the couch next to him. He has a film projector going and he's watching this

home movie of a young family which you are led to believe he is going to kill next. The family in the film is in their swimming pool. The camera moves in for a close-up of the woman's breasts. The killer looks intently at them and then over at the breasts of the contented-looking blind girl sitting next to him. He has the most depressed look of desperation on his face. She has been resting her hand on his leg and now she reaches over and kisses him.

The next scene begins with both of them lying in bed after having made love. She is sleeping peacefully but he is wide awake, lying on his back with a look of terror in his eyes. She is satisfied with the encounter. You know he desperately wanted to make love with her but now that it has happened he isn't satisfied.

Why not? After all, he needs that affection. She has given it freely but he is even more fearful of love now than before he met her.

He's not normal and he is painfully aware of it. He has become an evil monster and he knows he can never return to be the person he was before he began killing. He believes that no woman could ever love him once she was aware of what he has become. He can fake normalcy for only a very short time and then he has to revert to the monster persona because now that is who he has become.

In the next scene you see her getting off from work. She's standing in front of her house with a coworker who brought her home. She tells him goodbye but the stalker, who is sitting in his truck, watching her, believes he is watching a romantic encounter. He is so furious he rips the vinyl dashboard with his bare fingers.

Up to now he has been a very patient and skillful planner of his homicides. Now he just wants to kill. At this moment his mind is impervious to any thoughts other than executing her. When she goes into the house, he grabs the guy and kills him and drops his body by the side of the path. He grabs the girl and takes her to his place to terrorize her before killing her.

So how does this apply to your case?

I had killed and I was aware that my personality would never be the same as it was before the homicides. I was not normal and I would never be normal again. The urge to kill didn't leave me no matter how involved I got with Liz, her daughter, or her family. It was wonderful being with them and I could enjoy every minute of it, but I couldn't get rid of this urge. Like the killer in *Manhunter*, I wanted to believe I could be a happy and contented family man but deep down I know it could never happen. I couldn't be married and be confined to a home and family. That's why Liz and I had separate apartments.

There was a ritual to this man's killings in *Manhunter*. I understand you developed a ritual for your homicides as well.

Ah . . . Yes but I don't want to talk about that right now.

Chapter Thirty

Liz's Date

Let's go back to Liz's date. Liz mentions a guy she went out to dinner with. Did that have an effect on you?

> Yes, but I don't know just why it frightened me so much. My life had been filled with losses and I was used to it, but when Liz told me about this guy, I fell apart.

She said in her book that she went to dinner with him and you followed them, and she caught you pacing back and forth watching her. She asked you to leave, which you did, but you were waiting for her at home. You cried and pleaded with her because you were fearful of losing her.

> I was terrified of losing her. I told her how much I loved her. I just couldn't stand losing her.

Still, you wouldn't tell her you would marry her, even knowing that you could back out of it later had you wanted to.

> I couldn't. I just couldn't.

Ted, the incident with Liz going out with her friend from work took place in March of 1971. In July, Liz moved back to the University District. She said that everything was out of synch with you. You weren't staying overnight at her place as often and you seemed distant. What was happening with you?

> When she went out with that guy at work it devastated me. My love increased for Liz but my anger did as well—not only towards her but towards all women. But you read her book so you know that wasn't the only problem that occurred.

What do you mean?

> I had been preparing for my LSAT exams in order to go to law school. I took them that last fall. I scored low. I knew that others didn't score high the first time and I assumed my second attempt would be much better. However, my second set of exams weren't any better. This was my career they were messing with. It was my future. Without a law degree I had nothing. Every dream I had ever had was contingent on that law degree. Without that I would never have a chance for a career in politics.

I assume that you made some sort of a decision about what you would have to do to get around the exams. After all, you did get accepted into law school.

> I committed myself to achieving the highest grades possible to override the need for high LSAT scores.

And so you put a lot of time into your classes. How about your stalking? Trolling?

> I cut back on that. My classes and homework took up too much of my time.

But, in the spring of 1972, as you were getting closer to completing college, Liz became pregnant.

> Yes, and that made me very angry. She had informed me that her doctor recommended that she go off the birth control pills for a while to give her body a rest. I didn't want her to but I didn't want to appear insensitive. We decided that we would not have sex when she was ovulating. Still, she got pregnant.

Why did she have an abortion?

> We both decided that it would be best at that time, at least until I was out of school.

Did you not want to have a child?

> Once I got over being angry about her getting pregnant, I was ecstatic. I was going to be a father. You mentioned earlier how I seemed to fit in with her family. I really enjoyed Liz's parents. It was the family I never had. Liz's mother treated me like a favored son-in-law. You know that her father was a doctor?

Yes.

> He was very intelligent and he treated me with respect. He was willing to listen to my ideas, but not only listen; he was interested in what I had to say.

So did you want to have a family with Liz?

> Yes—and no. I had strong feelings both for and against it. The thought of raising my own child was very exciting. But I wasn't ready to settle down to family life and I wasn't ready to marry Liz. She was too insecure and she was becoming an alcoholic. I couldn't picture her as a politician's wife.

You and Liz were very close in the fall of 1969 but now your relationship was somewhat unstable. Was she changing or were you?

> I think we both were. But I guess I was the one that was changing the most. I wanted to have a wife and a career but I just couldn't picture Liz in that arrangement.

Ted, we now come to a time when your life began to seriously deteriorate. On one hand opportunities were finally coming your way. You had your own family and Liz's family and other people who respected and admired you. Still, your emotions were even more out of your control, you showed more serious judgment problems, and you were unable to hide these from others. Your success barometer was going up but your pathology and violence barometer were going up very fast as well.

Chapter Thirty-One

1972

You graduated from college with honors in June of 1972 and Liz gave you a yellow rubber raft, which becomes significant later in your story. One of your professors said that you had one of the most brilliant minds that he had ever seen. You got a full-time summer job with the Harborview Hospital Mental Health Center and in the fall you worked with the Governor Dan Evans reelection campaign. Liz still wanted to marry you. She was willing to put you through law school, and she agreed to wait to get married until you were ready. What more could you have wanted at that stage in your life? Everything was going your way. Even Marjorie came back into your life a year later and was willing to marry you. Everything that you had ever wanted was literally knocking at your door waiting for you to open it. Yet, in spite of all of these opportunities finally coming your way, something was going dreadfully wrong during 1972 and 1973 which prevented you from taking full advantage of them. In my report to the court I said that you weren't able to stay in any one job or activity for very long. You seemed to be looking for something and you weren't finding it. It finally all blew up on you in January of 1974 and from then until you were picked up by Sgt. Hayward in West Jordan in the fall of 1975 you had completely lost your ability to stop killing. In less than two years you killed 18 or more women. What happened?

> After I graduated I started getting cocky and I was spending less time with Liz. I can't put my finger on exactly what happened. I think the problems between Liz and me were part of it. Having my applications rejected from five law schools was part of it. A larger part of it, however, was that this thing inside of me was growing stronger and stronger.

But nobody was aware of it.

> I was very careful in covering my tracks. I developed compulsions to help control my obsessions. My apartment was immaculate and I even began cataloging my gas receipts. I was careful about hanging up my clothes in a specific order. I kept my secret life hidden from everyone.

But why were these compulsions necessary? Why, for example, was it important for you to keep your apartment so clean and to hang up your clothes in a specific manner? I remember Detective Jerry Thompson telling me that there was an equal distance between each hanger in your closet and not a speck of dust in your apartment.

> The compulsive traits helped me guard against errors and it provided structure to keep my stress in check a little better.

It didn't work very well for you did it? Tell me about your experience at the Harborview Mental Health Center in the summer of 1972.

> It was only to last the summer but it was the best option open to me at the time.

When we talked previously about it you said they assigned you intractable schizophrenics to work with.

> Yes. These people were impossible to help. Medication was the only thing which seemed to have any effect. Counseling didn't do any good because you couldn't use logic on a chronic paranoid schizophrenic.

I talked to a colleague of yours when I was gathering information for the psychological evaluation I was conducting on you. That person said that you were cold and distant with the patients.

> In some ways I guess I was. Working with these patients wasn't what I expected my job to be like. I was used to political strategies based on logic, but even with a depressed person the progress was slow. I was used to quick results. In politics you devise a plan, you set a strategy, and then you take action. If results don't come fairly quickly, you revise your plan and try again. You keep doing that until you achieve the results you are after. If the initial plan fails, you pull back and start with a new plan. Whether you are successful or you are failing, the results of your actions are quick and decisive.

But this was only part of the irritation wasn't it? Your fantasies were becoming more and more violent. Is that right?

Yes, they were. Now that killing was part of me, I wasn't afraid of taking a life.

What do you mean?

Well, assume for a moment that I had never killed anyone. Assume that I picked up a runaway who was going to San Francisco to be part of the hippy movement. We stop out on the desert somewhere to spend the night. I might try to make love to her and I might even rape her if that had been part of my fantasy life. But, even if I was absolutely positive that I wouldn't get caught, I still wouldn't kill her.

What would keep you from doing so?

Well, in that scenario, committing rape may have become part of who I was because I had fantasized about it so often. However, if killing had never been part of my fantasy existence then it would not have been part of my identity. Each of us naturally avoids doing things that are outside the range of who we believe we are and who we want to be. We deeply sense that it would radically violate the terms of existence that we have set for ourselves. We don't know what would happen if we were to violate those boundaries but we're afraid to find out. So most rapists, for example, aren't killers.

However, once a person has stepped over the line and has killed a victim, particularly if he enjoyed it in some way, this experience alters his identity. At first he is confused because he is not sure who he is any longer but he soon learns that while he may see himself as being different, for the most part he is still the same person he was. He also learns that he is able to hide this new part of himself from others. Killing is now part of his identity and the only thing that keeps him from doing it more often is that he doesn't want to get caught and lose his freedom.

But what he doesn't realize yet is that there's a good chance the urges will control him and he may not be able to avoid the killing cycles—no matter how much he wants to.

Let's back up. You worked with Ann Rule on the crisis line.

Yes. I wanted tension and action. It gave me the immediacy of results that I wasn't getting through my day job at the mental health center. It also gave me a chance to help others.

Ann Rule said that you talked a lady out of committing suicide. Is that true?

Well, one night while Ann and I were manning the phones, a lady called and said she wanted to die because her husband had left her and she was in severe debt. I could tell that she had been drinking. She scored high on the suicide lethality criteria we were using at the time so I felt there was some urgency that I help her.

How did you feel while you were doing it?

I felt wonderful. Remember, I had not succeeded in many notable accomplishments up to that time, and keeping a lady from committing suicide was a major victory for me.

So did you do it for the praise?

Not really.

Then why were you volunteering to work on a crisis line in the first place, let alone being concerned about preventing a woman from killing herself?

> Well, there were several reasons, not the least a desire to prevent death. I had already killed and there was still a part of me that didn't want to kill again. People talk about me as a monster that has a bloodthirsty habit of killing for the sheer pleasure of killing. It's not that way.

What do you mean?

> I constantly fought the urge to kill again but it came over me when I least expected it to. Once a person acts on a desire to take another person's life, that urge may never go away. It drives you. It's an unrelenting taskmaster. It has to be fed or it punishes you.

Are you talking about that side of you that you have been calling the entity?

> Yes. It's a powerful driving force and if you don't abide by its wishes you suffer incredible anxiety. You begin to feel a crippling helplessness. It's like being pulled out into the ocean by a riptide on a dark night. You feel completely alone. At times I would scream out at it to stop but that had no effect.

> I had never understood that when a person succumbs to a pathological urge the satisfaction is only temporary but the need for it may become per-

> manent. It's like an addiction to porn. Every time the person experiences stress, or boredom, or simply the biological urge for sex, the urge to look at porn returns. If a person enters the realm of violent porn, the urge for more of it grows stronger rather than weaker. If a person acts out these fantasies, a never-ending cycle of violence is created.

But killing . . . ?

> Killing is only an extension of that process.

Let's go back to your crisis line work. Ann Rule described you as a compassionate and motivated crisis line worker. You, however, are saying you didn't have compassion. I have respect for Ann Rule's observations and opinions; she is an acute observer of behavior. Talk to me about the seeming contradiction between what the two of you said.

> Well, first, I enjoyed working with Ann. She was one of the main reasons I kept going back as long as I did.

> But again, remember: Psychopathy is not a single all-encompassing process. A person can sell drugs to children, beat up prostitutes, or kill a competitor who is encroaching on his drug territory. At the same time, he can feel deep caring for his children, shed tears at the opera or symphony, and raise money for a charitable organization. And, he can man a crisis line.

But you were becoming a psychopath not only because you were stealing so frequently and easily without guilt or fear that you were going to get caught, you were becoming more violent in your consensual sexual activities.

Chapter Thirty-Two

Attempted Drowning

On July 4th, 1972, when Liz had gone to Utah to be with her family for the holiday, you took a woman who was a colleague from work to the Yakima River for a picnic. The two of you went swimming. Let me read you what she said:

> One time Ted took me on a picnic on the Yakima River. He asked me to jump from a tree into the river. I thought that was rather strange and I wouldn't do it. He became angry and he pushed me down into the river and held my head under the water. I couldn't get my breath. He repeated this 2 or 3 times. I thought, "We're the only ones around here. If I drowned, nobody would know."

When we got out on the bank we had sex. It was consensual but it was as if he was raping me. There was also a time that he choked me when we were having sex. At times he would space out. I often thought he was ignoring me. He told me he felt inferior to me and he wondered why I would ever go with him. He seemed to have no friends and he never spoke of any.[34]

Do you remember that incident?

Yeah, I remember it. Something came over me when we were swimming. I wanted to have sex with her and I knew I was going to be able to. After all, that's one of the reasons we had brought a blanket. But something came over me and I wanted to kill her. However, others knew that we were together so I didn't follow through with it.

I talked to another colleague of yours who mentioned a time that you and some others from work were at a restaurant. The issue came up about abortion and about illegitimate children. The lady I talked to said that you suddenly broke the glass you had in your hand. It shocked the others because they didn't perceive any anger in you prior to it happening.

I don't remember that. I think someone just made that up.

Ted, information from people who knew you during those years suggested that you were changing during 1972 and even more so during 1973. You were losing your ability to control your emotions and your behavior. The mask you had been showing to others was disintegrating.

You went out with at least two different women from the clinic where you worked. The one mentioned in incident in the river and the other said you put your elbow against her throat when you were having sex which made it very difficult for her to breathe. She said she called out to you several times but you didn't stop. She said it was as though you were unaware that you were doing it.

> I'm sure I was in a deep fantasy when I was doing it. I remember the incident because it seemed to frighten her. I apologized but it didn't seem to make any difference.

Chapter Thirty-Three

Homicide

Your temporary position at Harbor view ended and you obtained a job with the Dan Evans reelection campaign.

> That worked very well for me. I got to know Gover-
> nor Evans quite well and I became deeply involved
> in the work. He was reelected and I took Liz to the
> victory party.

In her book she said she was bored and she didn't fit in well.

> No, she didn't. We argued about that. Then in Janu-
> ary there was the Governor's Inauguration Ball and
> I took her to that as well. Again, she was bored. It
> was necessary that I interact with the key members
> of the party which prevented me from spending as
> much time with her as she wanted. She got angry

> and retreated to the bar and got drunk. She just wasn't what I was looking for in a politician's wife.

I assume that it was because of your association with the governor and other key members of his cabinet during that campaign that you got a position with the Seattle Crime Commission studying white collar crime. And then you worked for the King County Budget Office and you were appointed Assistant Chairman of the Washington State Republican Central Committee which allowed you to work closely with the chairman. In the late spring of 1973 you appear to have been doing fairly well. What happened?

> Liz went on a trip to Victoria, British Columbia with a guy. I tried to talk her out of it but she wouldn't listen. I told her she was making a big mistake but she turned and walked off. She said she was going to help him on his catamaran. I was furious. I had put up with her long enough; I was tired of her games. She professed she loved me and wanted to marry me yet she was going on a trip with this other guy named Greg.

Ted, there were two occasions during my previous interviews with you when I saw that rage in you. The first was when you spoke of this incident. It still bothered you so much that you weren't able to hold back from showing me your anger, even though you were aware that I was assessing you for the court. You said, "That was the last straw." What did you do when she went with him?

> I killed a girl.

Why? Why take that chance?

> I couldn't stop thinking about Liz being with that guy. I became enraged and I had to strike out somewhere.

How did this homicide come about?

I was in my apartment watching a baseball game on TV. I couldn't concentrate on the game knowing that Liz was with that guy. I remember the coach running out on the field screaming at the umpire for what he thought was a bad call. The camera zoomed in for a close-up of the coach and then it cut over to the stands to get the reaction of the public. The camera stopped on a beautiful girl. She was blonde, in her early twenties. She was yelling and screaming along with everyone else but there was something about her. I can't remember what it was but whatever it was it wouldn't let me take my eyes off of her. The camera returned to the coach but I wanted it to go back to that girl. I began to get sexually aroused but I was angry. I seemed to somehow make a connection between the angry coach and that beautiful girl. I began to fantasize about her. I wanted her. However, that was impossible.

I felt a change come over me. It seemed to start with a deep emptiness in my stomach. My breathing quickened and I became more nervous. Something was changing inside of me. It wasn't a rapid escalation of a sexual urge. It was slow, insidious, not something that I could push back down. The feeling moved from my stomach up through my chest and into my head. I could think and reason but the emotion was beginning to take over. I had felt the Entity off and on ever since I killed those two girls but not this strong. The feeling was too overwhelming to allow me to sit passively and watch the ballgame. I immediately knew the direction this emotional emptiness would take but I couldn't stop it. I didn't want to go out that night but the feeling was more definite and more powerful than anything I had experienced before that time. I fought the urge to leave my apartment.

I got up and I began pacing back and forth from one side of the room to the other. I kept looking back at the TV in an attempt to find a distraction and I turned the stations from channel to channel. I located a mystery and I tried to get involved in it but the pressure kept building inside of me.

Eventually, the storm occurring inside my body was so strong I couldn't fight it any longer. I had to go out. I headed out into the night reasoning with myself that I would only pick up a woman if she was hitchhiking and, since that wasn't very likely, I would just drive for a couple of hours until this ungodly feeling left me. Then I would come back. It was almost as if I was arguing with someone and when I returned back to my apartment I could say, "Well, I tried but the opportunity just didn't present itself." Then maybe this thing would back off and leave me alone for the rest of the night.

I put on my coat and climbed into my VW and began driving. I didn't select a particular direction. I just drove.

I had been driving for close to an hour when I saw a truck stop up ahead. To appease this thing inside of me I said, "I'll even go into the truck stop to see if any girls are trying to hitch a ride from there." I assumed this would satisfy the requirements of this thing since the chance of finding a girl there was extremely small. Then I would return to my apartment.

It would be too conspicuous for me to go in and look around for a girl, so when I went in I sat at the end of the bar and ordered a cup of coffee. I scanned the room and I was pleased that there were no girls there. I was satisfied that I could now go home. I left the café and climbed into my VW and I was about to turn back north when something inside of me said, "Just go a couple of miles farther. If you don't see anyone, you can turn around and be through for the night." All right, I thought, I'll go the distance. Then I can go back and go to bed.

I turned south out of the truck stop and I had gone only about a half a mile when I saw a girl hitchhiking. I was fearful and yet excited when I saw her. She was wearing jeans and she had a dark coat on. When I first saw her, I thought, "Please, don't stick out your thumb," but she did. I reasoned with myself that I would just pick her up and take her to some other truck stop down the road and let her go. I wouldn't hurt her.

I was very nervous when she was about to get into the car. "I'm going to Arizona. Are you going that way?" she said. Well, I wasn't, I thought, but I am now. She unzipped her coat and took it off, revealing a gray sweater. She climbed in and began talking about how she had run away from an abusive stepfather. She was going to visit a friend in Flagstaff after which she would decide what to do with her life. I can't remember just what I said but it seemed all right to her because she just kept on talking. Suddenly, I knew I was going to kill her.

I fought with myself, unsure of just how I was going to do it. I had thought of this moment for several months but I hadn't considered the most efficient manner in which to bring my subject under my control. Her initial warm smile was no longer apparent to me as she sat in the dark, talking, but her voice radiated her warmth. It was a sweet, trusting voice, but nonetheless I made myself believe that it was only a voice. It was a way of distancing myself from her.

It was surreal. As oncoming car lights illuminated the interior of my bug, I glanced over at her, as if to satisfy my doubt that the voice had an attached body. This crime would have been impossible had it been daylight.

Why is that?

With only an occasional glimpse of her face and a silhouette of her head she became less and less real to me. It allowed me to call her into my fantasy. I sensed myself making love to her.

I can't recall the moment I decided to strike and I can't remember actually doing so but I picked up a tire iron which I had between the seats and I hit her in the head, knocking her out. I pulled off onto a dirt road and drove a mile or so away from the highway. I took her out of the car and laid her on a blanket I had in the back seat of the car. Then I made love to her.

You raped her.

No, no, I didn't rape her. A person has to be conscious to be raped. She was still unconscious. I made love to her.

Then I held her close to me. For the longest time, I held her close to me. It was as if the two of us were having a very personal, intimate experience. You need to understand, at that moment, she was the person I had made love to so many hundreds of times in fantasy. All of the time I was physically with her, I was also with her in my fantasy. Half fantasy, half reality. But this time it was with an actual body. Not just an image. This fantasy with an actual body was more real than any intimate moment I had ever experienced.

I didn't know her name yet I felt I loved her deeply. I held her in my arms and gently rocked her back and forth. Again and again I told her that everything would be all right. It must be similar to when a hunter runs up to a deer he just shot and he realizes the deer is still alive. A friend of mine had this experience once. Unsure of just what to do next, he just stood there and, as he watched, the life left the deer. He said it was strange to stand over the deer as the life force left its body. It's a very personal experience.

As I held this girl, she began to come around. I knew that if she did live she would have serious damage to her brain. I couldn't allow that so I put my hands around her neck and ended any more suffering that she would have to go through.

What did you do next?

It was at that point that the fantasy came to an end and I was back in reality in the coldness of the dark night. Everything was silent and very still around me. I then gently laid the body on the ground and I picked up my blanket and left. I returned to the highway and drove south for a few miles and then turned around and went home.

Why did you drive further to the south rather than going back north to your apartment?

I don't know for sure. I had just gone through the most profound experience I had ever had in my life and I needed some time to adjust to it. Maybe that's why.

Did this homicide change you in any way?

As I look back on it now, it was like walking through a gate into a strange realm, knowing that you would never again return to that land that you had just come from. It was similar to when I killed the two girls back East. The former event changed me but this one solidified and made the changes permanent. After I killed the two girls in the East, I thought that I could avoid ever killing another person. But, after this one, I was fearful that I could never stop killing. This experience was so personal and so deep that almost every detail of it became indelibly fixed in my mind. It satisfied a hunger in such a profound manner that I am still drawn to her. When I allow myself to re-experience that memory, I can still feel her in my arms. As strange as it may seem, it's like a marriage. I bonded as strongly with this stranger in the few minutes I was with her as with any living woman I have known. I have never gotten over it and I never will. It was terrifyingly wonderful.

What do you mean?

I felt loved. I know it sounds strange to say that a person can feel love from a lifeless body but the love was not directly connected to the body.

That is strange, Ted.

It may sound that way. But remember, the victim is only a proxy for an image in a fantasy. Throughout the entire event, my mind is trapped in a fantasy. I earlier alluded to the killer in the film *Manhunter*. Do you remember how he had his home decorated? And the tattoos he had on his body? When he was at work he was in reality. When he returned to his home, he returned to his fantasy, to his more dominant personality. It was the fantasy that gave him life.

Well, it doesn't make any sense to me, but for the moment I'll take your word for it. Did it satisfy your hunger for that type of love?

No, rather than satisfying my deep hunger for love, it intensified it a thousand-fold. It activated my mind and my imagination. From then on I saw a potential victim in every attractive woman I came in contact with. Ever since then, the Entity has been the governing force in my life. It was as though this act fed him the blood he needed for total power and dominance over me. I was now aware that I was a serial killer in the full sense of the word.

What did you do when you returned to your apartment?

I went into a depression.

Why a depression and what thoughts accompanied the depression?

It was like walking into an empty house that was previously filled with happy voices and music and people coming up to you, telling you they are happy to see you. Now the house is dark. There is no furniture, no voices, and no music. Only a musty smell of decay. All life had left. I wanted to reach out and have somebody hold me and love me and tell me that everything would be all right. I wanted to tell somebody that I was sorry, but it was a secret that I would never be able to share.

When you were a child, what would you do when you felt a yearning for that love?

I would go to my mother.

It's interesting that you should say that. When you were a young child, you clung tightly to your mother.

She was all that I had. But I began losing her when my siblings were born. Over the years I had less and less contact with her.

Did you ever really have a mother? When you lived in Philadelphia as a small child you were told your mother was your sister. When you moved to Tacoma you must have been confused when this "sister" took the role of a mother. But then she had other children with your stepfather, a man that you didn't like very well. You have never had anyone, have you?

> That's not completely accurate. I had Liz.

No, you didn't have Liz. She tried again and again to give herself to you but she wasn't enough for you. No matter what you had in the form of education, recognition through political means, or relationships, it wasn't enough.

> I don't know where you're getting that from.

When you were recaptured after escaping from the jail in Aspen, Colorado, you called me.

> Yeah.

Do you remember the reason you gave for calling me?

> I hadn't talked to you for a while and I was curious about you impression of my escape.

Why? Why did you want to know what I thought about you having escaped?

> Oh, I don't know. Just curious I guess. What is it that you're getting at?

I recorded that conversation and I've listened to it several times since then. It was like a child saying, "Dad, what did you think of that home run I hit in the ballgame?" It was if you were seeking my approval, or forgiveness, or something.

Ted, you have never really felt the love of a mother or a father have you?

> Well, no.

What did you do in an attempt to get rid of the depression?

> I wrote letters to Liz. I told her how much I loved her. How much I needed her. And when we got together we both cried over it.

And she loved you enough that she was again hopeful that you would marry her and she was willing to wait until you were ready.

Chapter Thirty-Four

The Joy of Sex

According to what Liz said in her book, the rest of the summer seemed to have been better for you.

> It was, and in the fall I started law school at the University of Puget Sound. I wasn't happy with it because the buildings were old and dilapidated. However, it was law school and I was satisfied with that.

What did you do with your memory of having killed that hitch-hiker?

> I couldn't let it go. It was an obsession that dominated my thoughts.

Did you have any guilt about it?

No. I didn't want to take another life, but it was because of the problem I was having with the thoughts, not because of guilt.

What problem were you having with the thoughts? I understood you to say that the act was very exciting to you.

No, exciting isn't the right word. Skiing was exciting. This was a deep emotional experience akin to some form of love. I can't explain it beyond that.

Well, did you attempt to control it?

I watched women at night in the College District. I pretended I was having the same experience of love with them as I had with the hitchhiker. I perfected my ability to move around in the dark without being detected. I watched girls for hours at a time until I found one who was suitable for a good fantasy. I planned the technique by which I would capture and subdue them.

But that would only whet your appetite. The more you lived in that fantasy world the more your thoughts and emotions would be controlled by it.

Only to a degree. When I came back to my apartment after one of these, ah, nighttime events, I was excited and I felt completely alive. It got me out of my depression. In fact, I was so energized that I had a difficult time getting to sleep. I believed that this would satisfy my desires for the sexual love I needed so I wouldn't have to kill anyone again.

In the fall of 1973, you bought *The Joy of Sex*, a book on methods of sexual intercourse. One of the methods was bondage. As I remember, the author states that it is extremely sexually exciting to tie your partner to the four corners of the bed so that she is helpless when you make love to her. The author alleges that it is very close to rape and that it is very sexually fulfilling to both you and your partner. You still had that book when the police caught you in Salt Lake. Liz was willing to try it a few times but she then stopped it. What was so important about that book?

> It had become my sex manual. I thought that if I could get the sexual satisfaction that I needed from Liz then I wouldn't have to rape anyone.

Did it work?

> No.

Why not, do you think?

> Partly because she was a willing participant and not a victim.

And?

> And because a large part of the experience was in the hunt and capture. It's the darkness of the night. The hunt, the approach, and then the capture. Obsession is not simply a thought. It's the only thought. It's who you have become, and it completely controlled my life. When I was involved with my daily activities it was still a part of my reality but, when I was on a hunt, it was my only reality. It was not a place that I could visit and then decide if I liked it well enough to go there again. It was my life.

But I take it that it didn't work.

> It gave me excitement and energy but, by the fall of 1973, I was addicted to it. In all probability, I was

addicted to it several years before. The addiction probably started after Marjorie and I broke up.

Ted, I understand that you had to drink alcohol before you went out on a hunt.

Alcohol took away my inhibitions and it gave me courage. It was easier for me to talk to people if I had something to drink.

Chapter Thirty-Five

The Return of Marjorie

Ted, let's go back in the summer of 1973 once more. Marjorie came back into your life. You went to San Francisco and spent a week with her, and a little later in the summer she came to Seattle and spent a few days with you. Why?

> Actually, she had never fully left. Even after we broke up we continued to call each other from time to time and talk. But now I was desperate. I was hoping that if I could find a career and a woman to share it with that would give me the strength to resist the urge to kill and then maybe it would go away. Marjorie was still more than Liz of what I wanted in a politician's wife. Also, I was very self-assured and I wanted to see if I could win her back.

Liz thought that everything was going along all right between the two of you, and evidently you were able to convince Marjorie that you were still interested in her as well. Liz said you saw more of her now that you were back in school in the fall of 1973 but, at the same time, Marjorie was beginning to believe that you were serious about having a relationship with her. At times you even took Liz to class with you. It would be less than four months before you would begin your killing spree and, once it began, it wouldn't stop until Sgt. Hayward picked you up. What happened?

> When I killed the two girls back East, it was still largely an accident, but the intent to rape was definitely there. The killing of the hitchhiker was more thought out, planned. The earlier ones were quick, but with this last one I felt an intense love or, rather, possession that I had never before felt.

I still don't understand what you mean by love or possession. It's inconceivable that a person can feel love when raping and killing another person. It sounds psychotic. Yet, when I conducted a psychological assessment on you for the court when you were placed on the 90-Day Evaluation Program, you didn't demonstrate any characteristics of psychosis. I want to discuss the psychological testing a little later. For now, tell me about the love.

> You've heard rapists say that the fantasy of rape is more enjoyable than the real thing.

Yes, I have had several rapists tell me that.

> That's because in a fantasy everything is the way the rapist wants it to be. The victim says the right words, engages in the right behaviors, and shows the proper amount of love to the offender that he

>needs. In my homicides, I had a need to possess my victims and I was able to do this through fantasy.

What do you mean by "possess"?

>It was as if I now owned them. They were mine.

You talked earlier about the magnificent mounts of the bull and cow elk heads in the ski lodge in Aspen. A bull elk can have one or more cows. You spoke of him owning them. Is this what you mean by possessing?

>To some extent, yes. It's as if by taking the lives of my victims I would always have their souls with me.

But, Ted, you know that's impossible. First, you didn't believe in God so you wouldn't believe in the afterlife of a spirit; and, second, if you did believe in these things you would know that God wouldn't allow an evil person to have ownership over innocent and pure souls.

>I know that but, again, you do not understand the power of an intense well-practiced fantasy, particularly if there is dissociation going on during the fantasy. I didn't actually possess or own the spirits of my victims. What I possessed was the fantasy imagery and the emotion of ownership that went with it. I created that make-believe process of ownership within me. What made it so real and intense was that I had a human victim to do it with.

But why was it so necessary to keep doing it? Why was it necessary to actually kill anyone and, even with that, why wasn't one enough? To me, even the necessity of taking of one human life is incomprehensible. It's very difficult for me to understand why a person has to keep killing again and again.

A serial killer identifies with the pathology. He becomes the pathology. The pathology isn't part of him, it is him. It has become infused with his personality to the point that it has become his primary reason to live. It's not something that he can turn on and off. At first, his career aspirations and his relationships were who he was and the pathological thoughts were a secondary process that he could indulge in as the interest arose to do so. Now the killing and the sexual addiction pervaded almost all of his thoughts. His career and relationships were now secondary to the pathology. But, you have to understand, the thoughts of killing weren't in my mind all of the time. They would come from time to time, but I couldn't predict when they would take over my thinking. But, understand, I didn't completely give in to my pathology. During the fall of 1973 I spent time with Liz and her daughter, but I also nourished a relationship with Marjorie, hoping that she would help me find stability.

But all the time you were telling Liz how much you needed her and that she was the only one you loved, you were telling Marjorie that you were interested in getting back together with her. In fact, you were again able to convince Marjorie that you were on track with your law school aspirations and you planned on an exciting and fulfilling future and you wanted her to be a part of it. Was that just a ruse to gain revenge over Marjorie for breaking your heart?

It wasn't a ruse. In retrospect, it may appear to some that I was doing it just to get even with her, but that's not true. I was fully aware of what I had become and this was a desperate attempt to stop it. I loved Liz but she just didn't have the personality I was looking for in a wife. Marjorie did, or at least I thought she did.

What do you mean you thought she did?

I remembered her as she was when we were going together, and she still seemed like that when I visited her in San Francisco. I had idolized her and I still had this image of what she was like, and I expected her to still be that admirable person. But that was several years back and people change.

Chapter Thirty-Six

Living with Liz, Proposing to Marjorie

Ted, we now come to a very important event which appears to be a major turning point in your history. Liz and her daughter spent the Christmas season with her parents in Utah. Marjorie came to Washington and the two of you celebrated the Christmas holidays in a friend's condo. By New Year's Eve, Marjorie had obtained a proposal of marriage which she could take back to San Francisco, while Liz was telling her parents in Utah that the two of you were still going to get married, and you were only waiting to complete law school and obtain steady employment so that you could adequately support her.

Yes, that's true, but where are you going with this?

If this was accurate then I believe that you would have been satisfied with what you had accomplished. Liz was still supporting you and she didn't know about Marjorie, so you were safe there. You had deceived Marjorie and had obtained your revenge so you should have been able to have at least some level of closure. After all, the last laugh was yours. Under these conditions I would expect you to gloat over your success. However, you completely fell apart and you were never able to gain back any level of control until you were locked up. If it wasn't for the fact that you attempted to kill a woman three days after Marjorie left and kept killing without stopping after that, then I would have believed that my conclusion was accurate. But there's something I'm missing here.

This is probably a good time to talk about what happened during the Christmas holidays.

Chapter Thirty-Seven

Christmas 1973—The Fall

When I killed those two girls back East, I felt depressed and regretful about it. Extremely so. However, thoughts kept coming back to me about other things I could have done with those two girls had I had more time and wasn't so impulsive about it. Meeting Liz saved me from killing sooner than I did. However, my fantasy life was my retreat from failures and depression. There was so much I wanted in my life but it simply wasn't happening.

But, Ted, there were many positive events occurring in your life. You had completed college, you worked in political campaigns, you didn't have any difficulty in finding jobs, and now you appeared to have a fairly bright future ahead of you.

But my fantasy life was completely out of control.

In my employment I had learned about problems with police investigations so I became aware of the disposal of bodies. I learned about rape and the characteristics of rape victims. I had read every book or article I could find on serial killers and I read true crime stories. Through them I learned what the killer did wrong and I planned how I would do it differently. I was constantly running capture and homicide scenarios through my mind, sometimes for an hour or more at a time. I drove through areas in the mountains looking for places where I could dispose of the bodies of victims, and I monitored some of the areas to determine the flow of traffic. It had to be someplace that was not too far away because of the impracticality of transporting a body over a long distance.

There was a lady I talked to who worked with you at the clinic. She said that she would drive you up around Taylor Mountain and, when she asked what you were looking for, you said you were trying to locate where an aunt of yours lived.

Yes, but in fact I was scouting out locations for possible body dump sites.

But what does this all have to do with the Christmas holidays of 1973?

I was not only fantasizing about homicides, I was planning them . . . and practicing them.

Yes, go on.

I stalked women at night. I watched them as they walked across campus and through the university housing district. I pretended that I was going to attack them and I would mentally walk through the capture and the attack. Then I would plan on what I would do with the body and how I would cover up all evidence that I had been there. Then I would go back to my apartment, and sometimes I would imagine that I had brought the victim there and I would fantasize what I would do with her then.

This activity would sometimes go on for hours. It took up so much of my time and energy that I wasn't doing well in my studies. I often became frightened about the possibility of slipping and actually doing the crime rather than just fantasizing about it. In my more rational moments I tried to convince myself that it was only a fantasy and that I wouldn't actually do it. However, when I was depressed or frustrated about my relationships or my lack of work or my life in general, I found the urge to execute the crime to be almost overwhelming. As I look back on it now, I was grooming the Entity part of me to commit the crime. However, it appears that I was grooming another part of me as well.

What do you mean?

When I put myself into a deep fantasy, I was also partially dissociating as well. When the act had been completed and I stopped dissociating the other part of me would determine how to cover up the crime. It's as if one part of me was saying, "Let's do this criminal act because it would be so exciting." When the act had been completed—generally when I reached orgasm—I would come back to reality and the other part of me would say, "I wish we hadn't done that but now that it has been done, let's decide how best to get out of this mess." I was constantly practicing both parts in my imagination. Also, when I would go out at night, it wasn't to kill a victim but it was to see how close I could come to taking a victim without getting caught.

So, again, what happened during the Christmas holidays?

I was getting very close to committing another homicide. I was hoping that by restoring my relationship with Marjorie I would be able to turn my life around and get over these urges to kill.

But?

But it didn't go well with Marjorie. I acted as if I was confident and self-assured. I led her to believe that I was doing well in law school and that I had good prospects for the future. She wanted to get married the next spring, and finally I acquiesced and agreed to it. But then I realized that I didn't love her as much as I loved Liz.

I wasn't sure that I loved Liz that much either. Liz was very needy, and she was close to being an alcoholic. Marjorie was overly sensitive and easily angered. If I forgot tomatoes, Liz would be okay with it but Marjorie would have a tantrum. If I locked my keys in the car, Liz would accept it but Marjorie would fly into a fit of rage. Being the only child from a wealthy family she was used to getting her way. I couldn't stand up to her. Her personality was too strong for me.

On New Year's Day I drove Marjorie to the airport to catch her flight back to San Francisco, and then I rushed back to Liz and I told her how much I had missed her over the holidays and how much I loved her. Our sex that night was more passionate than it had been for a long time.

But?

But I was extremely angry and dejected. Liz saw the red parka and the new ski sweater that Marjorie had given me and she quizzed me about it. I told her my mother had given them to me, but she knew that my mother didn't have the money. She became distant and suspicious again because she thought I had probably stolen them. She came to my apartment and saw an antique clock I had on the wall and asked me where it had come from. I told her my mother had given it to me. Again, she accused me of stealing it, which in this case was actually true.

She was trying to be nice about it, but I could see that she was quite angry and didn't know just how to handle it. I became angry as well, and when I was like this I would usually go out stalking.

You never contacted Marjorie to let her know you weren't going to marry her, did you?

No. I didn't have the nerve. Fortunately, she was in California and I wouldn't have to face her in person when she began asking about it. Like I said, I couldn't stand up to her, not even over the phone. She finally called, which was almost a month later, and she asked why I hadn't kept in touch. She had told her family that we were getting married and they were beginning to plan the wedding. I was speechless and I couldn't answer her and she yelled and screamed at me and slammed down the phone. I was relieved that it was over.

So you weren't getting along that well with Liz, and Marjorie was in California thinking she was engaged, and you were caught in the middle of a bunch of lies. How did you react to all of that?

I had been watching a college student in the University Housing district so I ah . . . I ah . . . went to her place. I waited and watched until around 2:00 am. When I saw her enter her basement apartment I watched her undress and get into bed. She often left her curtains open. Ah, I had been watching her for a number of weeks and ah . . . ah . . . this time I decided that I would only watch her like I had done on other occasions. However, something came over me and I had to go in. I was very quiet and she didn't hear me. I opened the door and then quickly shut it so that the cold air wouldn't wake her. I had picked up a reinforcing iron from outside of her apartment and I went straight to her bed and I hit her with such force that I was sure I had killed her. When I later learned that she was still alive, I was happy about it.

I don't want to talk more about that one.

But Ted, why did you do it?

I really don't know. When I saw her lying there, I went into a rage and I began hitting her. It was as if she represented all the women who had hurt me.

What did you do then?

> I seemed to give up on myself. I had been fighting this urge to kill but now a change—a terrifying change—took place within me. It was as if I had stepped over that final line. Somehow, I knew for certain that I wouldn't stop killing. After that night the urge to kill never left me. But, you've got to understand, I never stopped fighting it.

But it began to affect your life in several ways.

> Yes. I couldn't focus on my studies and I began missing class. I was more nervous and edgy, and more distant. I felt more isolated and different from others.

In her book, *The Phantom Prince*, Liz said that during the early months of 1974 you and she weren't getting along very well. She said that on one occasion in March she returned to her apartment to find you there, in tears. She didn't know why you were crying but she welcomed the opportunity to offer you comfort. You indicated that you had dropped out of school because you couldn't concentrate and you couldn't apply yourself to your studies. She suggested that you reapply to the University of Utah Law School. You didn't tell her that you had already done so and were accepted for the fall of 1974. When you did tell her about being accepted, she asked if she was to come to Salt Lake with you. You were very vague about whether or not you wanted her to come.

> If she came then she would want me to spend my spare time with her and I knew I couldn't do it. I didn't want to commit myself to her.

You killed a victim about once a month and the police believed that there might be something about a cycle to the killings. Was there?

> I don't know. There has been some speculation that I might have had a bipolar disorder. I had mood swings and there were times when I was more depressed than at other times. Also, there were times when I was on a high. However, I was unstable and was drinking constantly, and with everything fading in my life, I was naturally happy when something good happened but then I became depressed when I was painfully aware the direction my life was taking.

Chapter Thirty-Eight

The Killing Contiues

Ted, on January 4, 1974 you attacked an 18-year-old woman in her apartment as she slept and you almost killed her. On February 1, you bludgeoned Lynda Ann Healy while she was asleep and then you took her from her apartment.

On March 12, you abducted 19-year-old Donna Gail Manson while she was walking to a jazz concert that was being held in the student lounge on the Evergreen State College campus in Olympia, Washington.

On April 17, you took 18-year-old Susan Rancort as she was walking across Ellensberg's Central Washington State College to attend a meeting. On that same night you were seen by a couple of other girls. They said you appeared to have an injury to one arm and you were asking for help to get your books to your car. Both of the girls who reported this said you led them from the library to a dark area beyond a railroad underpass to your Volkswagen. Each girl became fearful and ran. Neither reported it. Susan was the third one you attempted to abduct that night, wasn't she?

> It's been fifteen years, Al. I really couldn't say.

But wasn't that rather bold? Surely someone with an injured arm would attract attention in a library.

> I relied on the trusting nature of people and their willingness to help someone in need. Perhaps, but there aren't many students in a campus library at night and I was outside the library where I could observe the students coming out the door. If there was more than one student at a time I would turn away and appear busy.

On May 6, 22-year-old Roberta Kathleen Parks disappeared from the Oregon State University campus in Corvallis as she was going to have coffee with some friends.

On June 1, 22-year-old Brenda Carol Ball disappeared from the Flame Tavern in Burien, Washington, and then on June 11, 18-year-old Georgann Hawkins disappeared from behind her sorority house at the University of Washington. Georgann had been with others at a summer beer party. As she left to go back to her apartment she stopped and chatted for a few moments with a friend and then walked to her apartment. There was only about 200 feet from where she talked to her friend Duane to her place. The alleyway was lit and had he been watching he would have been able to see her walk the entire way until she was within a few seconds from her place. To abduct her in that location was extremely daring.

> That was the purpose of it. The greater the risk, the more intense the excitement. You have to remember that the objective was not the sex. It was the hunt, the capture, and the possession. And finally, the ownership.

But why take such a risk? You had proven your ability to do it, why did you have to do it over and over again? Each time you took a greater risk than the time before. Sooner or later you would get caught and then you would lose everything.

> But I didn't see it that way. I knew the dangers of detection but by then I felt I was beyond the capability of the police to catch me. Up to that time the police hadn't even come even close.

But you were becoming more and more careless, not only in the crimes, but in your life. You were becoming more distant from Liz. You dropped out of the University of Puget Sound Law School, and Liz and others detected that there was something seriously wrong with you. They didn't know what it was but they knew that something was happening with you.

> What do you think was happening Al?

I think you were losing control. Take the rafting trip on the Yakima River. Do you remember that?

> Yes, but I don't see how it is relevant.

Let's go over it anyway. It was during the summer of 1974. You, Larry Voshall, his date named Susan, and your date, a girl named Becky, planned a rafting trip down the river—in the raft that Liz had given you when you graduated from college. You had the one large rubber raft and a large inner tube connected to the back of it. Becky was floating on the inner tube and you untied the rope and then let it float away. It drifted over to a more dangerous part of the river and she became terrified.

>It was no big deal. There was no harm meant.

But Ted, you knew and the others knew that she couldn't swim. And when you were able to get her back to your rubber raft, you untied the top of her bathing suit, exposing her breasts to the others. You laughed about it.

>You are making it sound worse than it was.

It was said that you became very sullen and sulked after that. You had them steer the raft over to the bank and you said you were going to go down to get the car. You were within a 15-minute walk from your car but it took you more than an hour to get your car and drive back to pick them up. Your best friend Larry was with you and you acted so irresponsible. "Strange" was the only word they could find to describe your actions.

This event occurred on June 28th. It was only a little over two weeks after you killed Georgann Hawkins. A week later you took Liz down that river on that raft. You pushed her out of the raft into the water. She said that your face was expressionless, as though you weren't aware that it was her. In less than two weeks you kidnapped 23-year-old Janice Ott and then 19-year-old Denise Nasland from Lake Sammamish State Park in Issaquah, Washington.

Ted, there were 40,000 people at the lake that day. You walked among them, in the middle of the day, asking for someone to help you put a sailboat on the VW. You even introduced yourself to one of the women as "Ted." The brazen manner in which you kidnapped these two women was far different than the exceptionally careful person who beat that woman in her bed just six months before.

Tell me, why was it necessary that you kidnap and kill two of them on the same day?

> I hated what I was doing and I needed more and more risk and excitement to get my adrenaline going and to compensate for the depression and anxiety I was going through. I couldn't stop the killing so I had to allow myself to become completely absorbed in it. I was the Entity. The dissociation was complete. I wanted one victim to watch me kill another. I thought that this would give me a greater rush than anything I had experienced up to that point.

Did it work?

> Unfortunately, no. That's why I didn't do it again. However, there's another aspect to this.

What do you mean?

> There was a specific sense of fulfillment that I had to get out of a homicide and, if I didn't get it, the emptiness that I was experiencing in the hours prior to the homicide didn't go away. In the Lake Sam abductions, the first didn't give me what I needed. I don't want to talk any further about that.

What fulfillment were you looking for?

> I won't talk about that right now.

When the "Ted" composite came out in the newspapers it talked about a person named Ted and the metallic-looking Volkswagen that he was driving. Surely you knew that you were the person in the papers and that some people who knew you would likely call the police and finger you as a possible suspect. Did that bother you at all?

> Well, of course I had some concern, but I knew, partly from my studies of rape victims, that most rapists and serial killers don't get caught. There was a chance that the police would talk to me but witnesses are so unreliable that out of twenty to thirty people who might have seen me that day, it was unlikely that they would all agree on what they saw. And who would believe that an aspiring law student would be guilty of murder? No, it didn't bother me very much.

But weren't you taking a big risk? Why, for example, did you begin committing crimes in the daytime when you started during the nighttime?

> I didn't see that I was taking any risk at all. People don't look at other people very closely, and in any given period of an hour or more, they aren't likely to remember who they did or didn't see. I had been shoplifting for years and I was able to walk out of a store with some fairly expensive items, one of them being the eight-foot Benjamins tree that you spoke of. Sure, people are picked up shoplifting all the time, but I believe that most shoplifters don't get caught. I even had a lady hold the door open for me when I took that tree out of the store. Other store personnel saw me. I nodded to them and smiled. They were very pleasant towards me.

Chapter Thirty-Nine

The Salt Lake Period

You were becoming more and more of an empty shell of the person you had been. You had a good job during the summer of 1974 and you had a few friends. Your relationship with Liz was fair, at best, and you were making plans to move to Salt Lake. Since you didn't indicate that you wanted her to come with you, she said that she would stay in Seattle with her job and would possibly come down later.

She did come down ahead of time and found an apartment for you in the Avenues.

Yes, she did.

You left Seattle on September 2nd of 1974. You picked up a hitchhiker in Idaho and you killed her, and then you called Liz while you were still in Idaho. Why?

> When I picked up that girl, I didn't intend to kill her. But she was hitchhiking, it was a rural part of the country, and I believed that I wouldn't be caught. I was unable to resist killing her.

But why call Liz right after you killed her?

> It was the only way I could become grounded again. Talking to Liz brought me back to reality. I was the Entity when I killed a victim and, after it was over, I was still partially in that dissociated state. Talking to Liz and telling her how much I loved her brought me back to myself again. I didn't want to continue killing and I was hoping that by moving to Salt Lake and getting a new start—and getting away from Taylor Mountain—I would be able to get control over those impulses.

But it didn't work, did it?

> No. I killed three victims in the general Salt Lake area in the month of October.

Ted, what was your personality like when you moved to Salt Lake? That is, each of us has daily roles that we play in life.

> What do you mean by the roles I was playing?

Well, there is Ted the student, Ted the employee because you were working at least part time. There was Ted the boyfriend to Liz, and so forth. Finally, there is Ted the killer. To what extent did Ted the killer affect all of the other roles you had at the time? To begin with, tell me about Ted the student.

> Well, Al, as you know, I was in law school.

But you didn't attend your classes. Most of the students didn't remember you. For the most part, the professors didn't remember you. Law was your career choice, yet spending time in school was low on your list of priorities.

> No, you're wrong, law was my priority. That's why I went to Salt Lake.

It was my impression you went to Salt Lake because that was the only law school other than the University of Puget Sound that accepted you, and because you had to get out of Seattle.

> But by that time I had no power to fight the Entity. It was in my thoughts most of the time. I couldn't go into a store without seeing potential victims. As I stood in line at the checkout I would see a beautiful woman and I would approach her in my mind. I would start up a conversation based on something about her such as what she was wearing or what was in her shopping cart. I would ask for her help in some way, and when I got her to my car . . .

> But there's something you have to understand. I didn't go out with girls in Salt Lake simply because I had an overactive sex drive. I was hoping that by satisfying my sexual needs through legitimate relationships it would eliminate my need for a victim.

It appears that it didn't work.

> No. I discovered I could have enjoyable sex with a beautiful woman and still have to go out that night to hunt for a victim.

Chapter Forty

Ted Becomes a Mormon

I was shocked when you told me you had joined the Mormon Church in 1975. You initially told me that one of the primary reasons you didn't want to go to Salt Lake in the first place was because of the Mormons. You thought it would be too restrictive for you. What changed your mind?

> Well, part of the reason was because I was living among the Mormons and I thought that if I was a Mormon it would help me politically.

That doesn't make sense to me. Salt Lake at that time was less than 50% LDS. You weren't planning to live in Utah and you were aware of the anti-Mormon perception outside of Utah. I don't see any political gain by joining the Church. Come on, Ted, before joining the Church you went through weeks of missionary lessons. Weeks of listening to doctrine you didn't believe in and didn't intend to follow. You didn't believe in God, let alone have any interest in embracing a particular sect.

> I was trying to use the Mormon beliefs to help me gain some control over myself. However, evil can be very wonderful when you're engaged in it. It emotionally wraps its fingers around you and pulls you into its arms, and all the while it is moving through its steps towards a completion of some violent task you feel no reluctance to end it. You become part of its power. The closer you get to the target the greater the urge to hurry. Every part of your body is pushing, pushing, pushing towards the consummation of the act.

Towards capturing and killing a victim?

> Yes, and when the primal urge was awakened from its sleep, it would build so fast that I couldn't collect my thoughts quickly enough to stop it.

> People say they don't understand but they go through the same process almost every day whether it's with food, sex, or whatever.

But Ted, surely an urge for chocolate or even pornography is vastly different from the urge to kill.

> It's not a difference in kind but in degree. Any person who gets addicted to porn could also become addicted to killing if he allowed himself to become desensitized to it.

What does all this have to do with you joining the Mormon Church?

Once the evil act has been accomplished, the Entity, or whatever it is you want to call it, is satisfied and it goes back to sleep. That's when Mister Normal is painfully aware of what has been done. At times I felt extremely bad about what I had done. I wouldn't allow anyone to have control over my life, yet this Entity thing had more control over my emotions and my behavior than all the rest of the life-controlling forces combined.

This evil power had already destroyed much of who I was and who I wanted to be. I wanted to stop killing, so when someone told me about the missionary program, I agreed to listen.

And?

The two missionaries were friendly and they genuinely seemed to care. I liked what they were offering and I hoped it would give me the control I needed to stop. If there was a God then maybe He would cause me to stop killing. After all, it was His children that I was killing. I really did want to stop. An evil personality is a very heavy burden to carry.

Did it help to join the Church?

It helped when I was with the missionaries or when I went to church but, when I was away from them, the old urges came back. Also, when I saw a beautiful girl in church, I had to fight the fantasy that I automatically began to have about her.

When I killed another girl I decided that religion wasn't going to help so I gave it up altogether.

On November 8, you attempted to abduct Carol DaRonch but she was able to escape from your Volkswagen with the handcuffs still attached to her wrist. Later in the evening you went to Viewmont High School and you kidnapped and killed Debra Kent. Why two victims in the same day? And why Viewmont High School? There were several people who saw you there, in the building, trying to get someone to help you carry books out to your car. If anyone had taken a close look at you, you could have been easily identified.

> I was desperate. When Carol DaRonch eluded me, the drive was still active, and I could only satisfy it by successfully finding a victim.

Ted, let's talk about the phenomenon you call the entity. At the time of the homicides, was there some type of supernatural personification inside you that forced you to kill these women? That is, was it Ted Bundy who killed these women or was it some evil personage that temporarily possessed your body?

> I wish I knew the answer to that, Al. If I did, it would make my present circumstances much more comprehensible. What do you think it was?

Well, you didn't believe in God or the devil or in an afterlife and I have never heard you speak of demonic possession. I have to assume that whatever this entity was, it wasn't a supernatural being from some spiritual origin or some altered reality.

> Supernatural, no. However, it most definitely was an altered reality. It was me but at the same time it wasn't me. There was no loss of consciousness. It wasn't like the case of a multiple personality disorder where one personality takes over and, when this part goes away, the host personality has no

> awareness of what this other personality did when it was in charge. I was aware of what I was doing. Only, I couldn't stop myself from doing it. There was a shift in my consciousness from reality to this partially dissociated state that I habitualized through fantasy. The part I played again and again and again during this dissociated state became the Entity. The only way I can explain it is that by creating and then nurturing this self-imposed altered state in my mind, I was utilizing a different part of my brain. It's as if this process occurring in my brain became compartmentalized from my more normal daily functioning.

How can that happen?

> I don't know for sure.

Is it possible, then, that the building of a memory cluster can become so strong that once it is triggered you have to live out—or act out—the sequence until it comes to its natural conclusion? The entity, then, may not be a personage but an overwhelming drive or addiction that, once triggered, seems to take on a life of its own.

> That could be.

Still, you were fully aware of what would happen to you and your career if you were caught. Prior to you being caught and found guilty of these homicides, many people who knew you couldn't see any indications that you didn't have morals or ethics. Did you have any ethics?

> Of course I did. However, they were more for show than genuine.

Then why didn't they stop you from killing?

> If I haven't already said it, let me say it now. The urge to kill or rape wasn't always present. It came in cycles. People think we walk around constantly lusting after some woman. That's simply not true.

> However, when the urge was triggered, a dramatic change began to occur. It was like listening to a station on the radio when another station gradually appears. As this new station gets louder, the first station gets softer. It doesn't take long before the second station completely drowns out the first one. It's not like having two stations blaring at the same time with one being stronger than the other. As I began to feel sexually aroused, I *had* to have a victim and I couldn't rest until I had achieved it. And as strange as it may seem to you, it didn't *feel* wrong.

> This belief and emotional justification didn't leave me until I had killed a victim. And, no matter how much I reasoned with myself about how wrong it was to continue doing it, I couldn't stop. It was as though my sexual release was completely contingent on the act of killing and possessing a victim. No other mode of sexual release would even begin to come close to satisfying me.

Again, what do you mean by possessing a victim?

> Think of it as a simultaneous combination of two drives, a sexual need for pornography combined with the feeling of excitement and power when you are looking at a prize elk through the scope of your rifle. When you bag the elk, you can't just walk off

and leave it there. You have ownership of it. You have to possess it. You may mount its head on your wall, and every time you look at it you can remember the exhilaration you felt when you shot it. The hunter doesn't go around crying, "Oh dear, I just killed that elk! What a horrible thing to have done!" No, he has a friend take several pictures of him by the side of the elk. He puts the pictures in an album and he shows them to anyone who comes to his home. He places the mounted head on his wall for everyone to admire. He's proud of his prize elk and he never tires of talking about the hunt, the stalking of the elk, and then killing it.

I understand that, but what about the sexual drive? What part does that play in all of this?

The sexual drive is one of the most powerful drives a person can experience. The drive for achievement is another, and hunting is a very powerful achievement drive. If a person experiences both drives at the same time, the result is a very anxious person who is obsessed until he finds satisfaction. Following an attack on a victim, there is a sexual release and that aspect of the super drive is satisfied. However, he can't mount the victim's head on his wall and he can't take pictures to put in an album. He may take souvenirs . . .

Like their decapitated heads?

Or anything that belonged to the victim to help him relive the experience.

But why take the chance?

Once I killed a victim and I was back in reality—the intruding radio station leaving my radio and the original station now blaring at me—I had a number of strong mixed feelings. I felt very bad for what I had done.

You felt guilt?

Well, not guilt really. I knew I had to stop because it would destroy my career. I felt bad because it had happened again. I really did want to stop. But, as I said earlier, killing the victim bonded me to her.

What about possession?

I didn't possess her body or her soul but I possessed the memory of her. I savored that. You need to understand, there not only has to be a justification for doing the act in the first place, there has to be a justification following the act for having done it. Holding on to the memory of the event and feeling very close to the victim was, in a sense, a justification for having done it. It was as if I was telling myself that the bonding between me and my victim made the killing all right.

You have talked very little about this. Why?

It's all I have left of my contact with my victims. It's similar to a person who has a number of stolen fine art paintings in his basement. They are for his eyes only. If he lets it out to others that they are there, they cease being his alone. There are things I will never tell anyone about the murders.

Chapter Forty-One

The Capture, Evaluation, Sentence

The time finally came that you were caught. It seemed that you were incapable of stopping your crimes.

That's what I've been trying to tell you.

When the people in Seattle heard of your arrest, they were very surprised. They couldn't believe it. Many believed that Salt Lake had made a dreadful mistake. In their minds, there was no way the Ted Bundy that they knew could possibly have been responsible for killing anyone. But you were found guilty by Judge Hansen and you were sent to the prison for the 90-Day Evaluation.

These evaluations made you very angry, didn't they?

Not at first, no. It's just that they seemed to go on and on and on. When I thought I had cooperated enough, there were more tests and more doctors to see. Let's see, there was you—the person I spent most of my evaluation time with—and Dr. Austin, the psychiatrist, and then two other psychologists, a Dr. Roe and a Dr. Howell.

Let's go over the findings. First and foremost there were no serious indications of depression or of an anxiety disorder; you scored within the normal limits on the tests measuring these traits. Most people can't understand how a serial killer can have a severe need to kill women yet not have a mental illness. You were locked up in a prison setting, your law studies had come to a halt, and there was a possibility that you could be spending a few years in prison. Still, you were saying in the tests that you didn't have any depression or anxiety. Ted, for someone so intelligent, you made some gross errors.

What do you mean?

If you had indicated you had some depression and anxiety, it would have fit a college student who had been wrongfully convicted. However, by saying you had absolutely no anxiety and no depression, it suggested that you were either not innocent or, if you were innocent, you had a superhuman ability to not let it bother you. Or that you were a psychopath who didn't feel guilt when you harmed people. You were facing several years in prison yet you were saying that it didn't bother you. Ted, you had already demonstrated your ability to manipulate and fake but you were not able to do it in the psychological tests I gave you. The only conclusion I could come up with was that you were guilty of not only the DaRonch case but probably the killings as well.

Well, several things were going on. First, as I told you during the assessment, I have never been

> bothered by fear. I don't think about tomorrow. I live for the moment.

Even though you weren't bothered by fear—which by the way I absolutely don't buy—you would have come out better in the psychological assessment had you indicated that you were at least somewhat anxious about the whole situation. Then you would have appeared more normal.

> You don't believe what I said about having no fear?

No, of course not. Detective Jerry Thompson told me that you appeared increasingly distressed as he got close to having sufficient evidence to arrest you. You were calling him daily for updates on your case. You certainly showed fear then.

> Well, the psychological assessment was a challenge, a contest between you and me. I felt that you were trying to find something to tell the court that would put me in prison, and I wasn't going to let you do it. Dr. Austin and the other psychologists didn't attempt to contact people in Salt Lake or in Seattle, and I couldn't understand why you did.

But if there wasn't anything negative to find, why would you be so concerned about it?

> My behavior had seriously deteriorated over the previous couple of years. If you kept turning rocks over, sooner or later you would find something underneath one of them.

> I'm curious. Why did you spend so much time with my evaluation?

Because you were so guarded and evasive. I remember the first day I saw you. You walked toward me with your hand extended and a big smile on your face and said, "Hi, I'm Ted Bundy. You must be Dr. Carlisle." You acted more like a person running for a political office than one who was about to be evaluated for a possible prison sentence.

And, as the testing progressed, there were various subtle indicators of pathology that I wanted to follow up on.

> What do you mean? What were these "subtle indicators"?

On straightforward test questions asking about anxiety and depression, you denied having those emotions.

> But, remember, I didn't believe that the prosecutors had a case against me.

But Judge Hansen had found you guilty and there was a good chance that you would be given a hard number.

> Maybe so, but it was based on such thin evidence that I expected to be put on probation. I would have continued with my law studies while fighting to have the case overturned.

You liked the prospect of being able to fight your own case.

> Of course. Five law schools had turned down my application for their program. I didn't do well at the University of Puget Sound, and now I had the opportunity to practice law, even if it was in defense of myself. I was totally confident that I could get the case overturned. So, when faced with the psychological and psychiatric evaluations, I wasn't anxious because I anticipated a favorable outcome. After all, I had been stealing from stores for years. I had killed many women but I had completely evad-

ed detection. It wasn't the police who caught me. It was my own carelessness at Lake Sam when I introduced myself as Ted.

Now I know you're going to ask me why I was so careless. It was partly because of the urgency to satisfy my need. And, the possibility of detection didn't enter my mind.

And I was able to beat you in the psychological evaluation. Even you couldn't tell the court that I had the personality of a killer.

What did you see in the tests, anyway?

Well, first, it was obvious to me that you were faking. On the Bipolar Psychological Inventory you indicated you didn't have any anxiety, depression, or anger. However, there were a couple of inmates who informed me that you would pace back and forth in your cell, talking to yourself. You appeared very stressed to them. Another inmate saw you standing by the window at the end of the corridor, spaced out, as if you were in another world. He said you appeared very nervous or depressed.

But you said in your report that my personality fit the crime. What made you say that?

There were several things, actually. First, your scores on the true-false tests indicated you were faking, and I reasoned that if you were innocent, as you said you were, you shouldn't have had anything to hide. I wondered, then, what you were trying to keep me from seeing and why you were able to do it so well. Your answers were too smooth, as if they had been rehearsed. You stumbled twice, as I remember. One was when I asked you of your belief in an afterlife. It wasn't the answer you gave that tripped you up but the hesitancy, the difficulty you had in coming up with *any* answer. Also, you frequently contradicted yourself.

> No, I didn't. Why do you think I contradicted myself?

When I asked you about a year in elementary school, you would initially say that it went very well. However, when I asked you about the next grade you commented on how it was much better than the prior year, the one you had just talked about, that you had said had gone so well.

Then there were the people I contacted who had known you.

> Why did you contact them? None of the other evaluators did.

The best way to understand a person is to see him through the eyes of others who have dealt with him over the years. There were several who said there were two sides to your personality, a good side and a strange side. There was the girl who told me about you choking her during sex and she had a difficult time bringing you out of your reverie. Another was the girl who said you held her head under water three times when the two of you were swimming in the Yakima River. Then there was the landlady who said that you borrowed expensive China from her to host a dinner for Marjorie and that you often used a fake British accent. There was a person who said you would come to your room in the apartment house by a ladder instead of going through the front door. And then there was the story about the raft trip in which you untied the bikini strap of your date and let it fall, exposing her breasts to your good friend and his date. And when your date was floating in a rubber tube in back of your raft, you untied the rope and allowed her to drift into rough waters knowing that she couldn't swim. All of this told me that there was a strange and possibly violent side to you.

> You showed me some pictures and had me tell stories to them. What was the purpose of that? I'm still trying to figure that out.

You're talking about the projective tests. I used the Thematic Apperception Test, commonly referred to as the TAT. This was the test in which you were given a series of pictures and you were asked to tell a story to each of them. While none of your stories were so blatant of pathology that they could hold up to a cross-examination in court, most of them reflected what you were going through in your life at the time.

> For example?

Well, one of the cards is of a man and a woman. The man appears to be leaving and the woman appears to be trying to hold on to him. Let me read what you said:

> Both of them have interesting expressions on their faces. The woman's is of admiration almost and of passion. The look on the man's face is one where he looks eager and confident. He may be leaving for some—for a trip, or an adventure and she, proud of what he is about to do, wants to kiss him one more time before he leaves. He is dressed in the shirt of a working man but may not have his tie on. They're married and they haven't been married long but she appears to be very much in love with him and he appears very eager to do what he what he had to do because he had that confidence and he was ready and he came back and now with that job off his mind, he could turn to her and have the same love in his eyes that she had for him.

> Did I really say that?

Yes, you did. I recorded it on tape. Remember?

There are several items in this story that we could talk about but an obvious section is about the woman who has a look of admiration and passion on her face. She is proud of him. This may be Liz and her love for you and her pride in you going to law school. The sentence, " . . . she appears to be very much in love with him and he appears very eager to do what he has to do" along with, " . . . he came back and now with that job off his mind, he could turn to her and have the same love in his eyes that she had for him," is a very close fit to the killing drive, and when it was over you could come back to Liz and show her the love you had for her. You did this several times, didn't you?

> But in the picture, she was proud of what he was going to do. You're not suggesting that she was proud of me going out to kill someone.

She was proud of you going to law school. But this "adventure" wasn't law school, was it? You didn't do well in law school because you were too deeply involved in your homicides. When the urge came on you to go after a victim, you couldn't rest until "that job" was off your mind.

> All right, you have a point.

Ted, there was one particular story that you told me that brought tears to your eyes. One of the TAT cards is blank. I asked you to make up a picture and tell a story to it. Let me read what you said:

> Well, the picture that's in my mind the most all the time is a picture of a girl I love very much. But it's mostly of the picture of her and one

that occurs most often in my mind is a picture of her kneeling, cleaning the oven. Just standing there in the doorway watching her clean the oven when how in spite of all the grease around her elbows, the smudges on her face that I really cared for her, knowing that I could take her any way she was, dirty or clean. In that picture of her when I came over to her and how happy we were to see each other. And I only hope I know how it ends.

It's obvious that you gave this story to try to impress me about what a wonderful loving relationship you had with Liz. However, it wasn't at all true, was it? She was in Seattle working to help support you while you were making love to—and killing—women in Salt Lake City.

There is one part of the story I want to ask you about. Of all the things you could have said about her, you placed her in the kitchen cleaning the oven. When I had a psychologist friend of mine read that story, he asked if your girlfriend had had an abortion. Ted, I don't think that you had ever fully adjusted to losing your child when Liz got an abortion, even though the two of you agreed on it.

It was something that we had to do but I felt bad about it. I couldn't marry her and I didn't want my son to be a bastard child like I was. I eventually wanted a family, but not then.

Chapter Forty-Two

Colorado and the Escape

Ted, you were found guilty of the attempted abduction of Carol DaRonch and you were sentenced to the Utah State Prison. Utah gave you up to Colorado to pursue homicide charges against you for Caryn Campbell. You were confident of beating the charges there and yet you escaped. Why?

> Because I thought I could do it. After all, except for the one charge in Salt Lake, no police agency had been able to catch me in any crime that I had committed. It was natural for me to believe that I could get away with this as well.

Tell me about your escape from the courtroom in Colorado. Why did you take that chance? When you called me you said that you were more confident than ever that you would win your court case in Colorado. You also believed that the DaRonch case would be overturned. Yet, you were already planning your next escape. You called me. Why?

> Well, we hadn't talked for a while and I had a credit card. I called other people besides you.

I'm aware of that. But why me? I had written a damaging report on you for the court. I would have thought that you wouldn't have wanted anything to do with me at the prison. Yet you were willing to continue talking to me. It wasn't a complete surprise when you called me from jail following your first escape.

I have always felt that you were a very lonely child.

> No, that's not right. I have always had friends.

You had some friendships but no close friends, and that's sad because you were so friendly. Many people seemed to like you.

When you were with Liz's family you were part of their activities, including helping her mother in the kitchen, going hunting with her father—except that you didn't want to shoot animals. Liz even said that you didn't like hurting animals.

People who knew you felt you had a compassion for the poor and the disadvantaged.

When you were in jail you wrote countless letters to people. You wrote a sixteen-page letter to Liz. I remember a very lengthy poem you wrote to Ann Rule. With your permission, she sent me a copy of it. There was a very impressive aspect about you. You were an immaculate dresser in your expensive clothes. Classical music was your favorite genre.

When you called me from jail, you asked for my impression of your escape. You even complimented me on my correctness of the psychological report I did on you for the court. And, even when you were caught in Florida, you wouldn't confess guilt to the detectives, yet you spent lengthy periods of time chatting with your jailers. You reminded me of a little boy hungry for recognition and acceptance.

Ted, if you were so confident about your acquittal, why did you take a chance and escape? Surely you understood that an escape would only confirm your guilt in the minds of most people.

> It was motivated solely by the belief that even if I was acquitted of all charges, Washington would never allow it to rest. Public opinion was against me on these crimes. People had become paranoid about anyone who might hurt their daughters and, even though I was entirely confident that all charges against me would eventually have been dismissed, it would have taken several years to fight my case through the courts. By then it would have been too late to have a public life in politics. Society needs somebody to blame and the police and the press pointed to me as their best candidate.

So did you escape to start a new life?

> Of course. My intent was to start over with a new identity, and of course I would have to alter my career plans. I believed the malignant condition which caused me to kill women was, as it were, laid to rest. There was little doubt in my mind that I was finally in control over those destructive urges.

But what happened?

> As long as I was in the protected environment of the legal system the opportunity to act on the evil

impulses was muted. Essentially gone. The need was not active.

What do you mean by the need not being there?

I was actively fighting the legal system and I was winning. The sense of power I had over the police was intoxicating, and you must understand I was inebriated when I committed my crimes. There was no chance to obtain alcohol when I was locked up. My jailers watched me too closely. I still had fantasies of killing but the chance of overt behavior was nonexistent. This was a significant departure from who I had been, and I was deluded by the inactivity of the Entity.

It changed after you escaped.

Honest, Al, I fully believed that I had control over this thing inside me. Since I hadn't felt him completely taking over my body for some time I thought that I was deconditioned. In my view, he was gone and, as long as I was actively engaged in achievement and relationship pursuits, the occasion wouldn't reoccur for him to become active again. My life in the future would be a significant departure from who I had been.

So what happened?

Well, I guess that's the million dollar question, isn't it? All I can say is that, although I was exhilarated that I was free, I felt more alone than I had ever felt in my life. I had nothing. Absolutely nothing. No job. No money. No friends. I couldn't ask a girl to go out with me because I had no car and no clothes.

I wanted to talk to my mother but if I called her it would only make her worry even more about me.

You went up North.

Yes, but it was cold. A nationwide manhunt would be put out on me; I was paranoid of every police car that came towards me. I was fearful that I would run into someone who knew me. Sooner or later someone would recognize me so I had to change my identity. The North was too depressing for me so I came to the South. I wanted to be around a college campus. It was risky but, then, the risk was great anywhere I went.

It has been speculated that you selected Florida because of the high rate of executions there.

I had no desire to be apprehended, let alone to be executed. Some have speculated that I had a sub-conscious desire to be caught.

Did you?

At one time I would have said absolutely not.

Did you change your mind?

Not really. However, there were times that I, uh—don't take this wrong—but there were times that my desire to stop my destructive behavior was so strong that I, uh, might have desired it—but only subconsciously. There was never a time that I wanted to turn myself in. I never wanted to be ap-prehended.

Did you ever attempt suicide, or have any thoughts about want-ing to die for your crimes?

Oh, hell no. I'm a survivor.

But a very destructive one. You survive by killing others. Death is life to you.

You have no right to say that, Al. That's just not true.

But isn't it true? Weren't you more likely to seek out a victim when you were angry and depressed? When you raped a victim, didn't you feel renewed power? When you possessed your victim, didn't you feel love that had utterly eluded you throughout your life? You didn't want to kill but it appears that you couldn't exist without doing so.

That sounds sick and deranged when you say it that way.

Ted, you were sick and you were deranged. When you allowed the entity to develop within you, you gave up your freedom to make common decisions about your life. You gave up all of your ability to be a normal human being. Every child wants to have a career and a family. You gave all of that up once you crossed over that line.

But doesn't everyone who gets heavily involved with pornography give up some freedom? Still, they function normally in society.

It depends on your definition of normal. A person heavily involved with pornography has given up his ability to have an intimate and deeply bonding relationship with his wife or partner. Sexual excitement replaces mature love. The person becomes enslaved to his desires and he is never fully capable of appreciating his wife for herself alone. He is constantly seeking the next level of sexual excitement.

Ted, when you got to Florida, what kept you from settling in and working towards another career and another relationship? You had been there for only about a week when you began killing again.

> When I was up North, the urge to kill a woman became very strong. I thought that I was over it and it terrified me when it came back. I started drinking, thinking that if I was drunk that I wouldn't have the mental capacity to carry out a crime. But I didn't want to escape into alcohol. I was afraid that this urge to kill would never go away.
>
> I thought that if I went to a warmer climate and I was by a campus that it would be less depressing and I could possibly get back in school, under another identity, of course.

But . . . ?

> When I got down there I felt better but then the desire to have a victim was even stronger. I was extremely hungry for a woman but I knew that a normal sexual experience would never satisfy me. The Entity had been awakened and only the death of another victim could satisfy him. I can understand the alcoholic who returns to whisky after having have given it up for several months. He goes off the deep end and gets extremely drunk. I've talked to guys in here who were able to stop drinking and they knew that if they took another drink they wouldn't be able to stop again.

So you began prowling again?

I thought that if I raped a woman it would satisfy me and I wouldn't have to kill her. There had been times that I allowed my victim to go free after a rape. There were even times when I picked up a girl hitchhiking and I didn't try to rape her.

But this time you couldn't stop yourself.

Honest, Al, I didn't want to kill another girl. I really didn't, but you've got to understand that when those destructive urges overtake you, they catch you off guard. I didn't have time to change when I was in prison and I hadn't prepared myself for this drive to return.

Didn't you continue to fantasize about rape and killing when you were locked up?

Well, of course I did but it was in a controlled environment. Not being able to act on those desires caused me to believe they were controlled. I didn't anticipate that they would come back and, when they did, it made me very fearful. My objective was to change my identity, earn some money, and go to another country, someplace like in South America or Australia.

Then why take the chance of raping again? You were in a college town and you could have found some girl who would have been willing to have sex with you. You never had any difficulty finding someone.

At that point, sex was not enough. However, when I started prowling and I saw that girl dancing naked in her apartment, I decided that I would only rape her. If she told the police that she was dancing naked and some guy came in and raped her, they wouldn't likely do anything about it.

That was your intent. What happened?

I had been drinking and I had an overwhelming urge to not only rape her. I knew that I would kill her and it would start all over again. I felt that I would never stop. I couldn't stop. It didn't matter if I went to Australia; it would be the same there. I couldn't stop and I knew it.

So how did you select the Chi Omega House?

I don't know. It just happened.

What do you mean?

The girl in the apartment had left to go somewhere so I walked around for a while. Something distracted me and when I looked over I saw a girl go into the back of the Chi Omega House. I was so detached from everything that I just reacted. I don't remember a lot about what happened. I picked up a piece of wood and I went in the same door the girl had gone into. I don't want to talk any more about that. You know what happened after that.

But that wasn't the only girl you killed that night was it?

I was so angry at myself and everyone else that just one would never be enough.

Will you talk about the Kimberly Leech case?

No. That one was so traumatic for me because I was very detached from myself when I did it. I went

> beyond my boundaries. I didn't want to hurt some-
> one that young.

But you selected an elementary school. Surely you were aware of what you were doing?

> I was and I wasn't. I had to find a victim and all of
> the college-age girls were paranoid of strangers. I
> couldn't approach one of them but nobody would
> expect an attack on a young girl.

When you were caught and you were taken to the police station, a detective called and asked if I would come to Florida to talk to you. He said you were very distraught and seemed on the verge of confessing. He thought that I could possibly play a part in getting you to confess.

> Would you have done that?

Oh, certainly.

> But you didn't come.

You quickly gained your composure and you stopped talking to them. The point I am making, or rather, the question I'm asking is: Why were you falling apart?

> The Chi Omega incident, and more particularly kill-
> ing that little girl, affected me more profoundly than
> any experience of killing that I had ever had. I hated
> myself. I couldn't sleep. I was suicidal. I couldn't
> escape from the memory of that little girl. I wanted
> to die but I couldn't kill myself. I wanted that cop to
> shoot me.

But you regained your composure?

> Yes.

And, once again, you were in your element. You took on your own defense against the state. You were admired by the other inmates here in prison. You had a girlfriend who stood by you and proclaimed your innocence. You were even able to marry her by pulling a fast one in court before the judge, the lawyers, and millions of people who were watching on television. You were able to have a child by her, even though you were locked up in prison.

[At this point, an officer raps on the window informing me that I have five more minutes.]

Well, I see that our time is almost up. There's one thing that I don't fully understand. You recently contacted Dr. Bob Keppel, a retired detective who had spent years investigating your case. You confessed the details of your crimes to him. You contacted Dr. James Dobson from Focus on the Family and asked him to do a taped interview of you. In the interview, you publicly admit to your crimes and you blame it on pornography. It is my opinion, and I'm sure most people would agree with me, that this was an attempt to get a stay of execution. Did you think you had a rational expectation of that working? The whole thing seems like another manipulation, except for the fact that there have been occasions when it appeared that you have tried to change. Or was I wrong?

> There have been times when I've wanted to change but I was never successful at making it happen. There were other times that I felt so much like God that I didn't have any desire to change. That's a powerful experience. However, there is always a let-down. The aftermath of crimes like mine is a sense of being more evil than can possibly be put into words. The only way I could live with who I had be-

come was to go with the evil and find ways to justify it. Since talking to religious people who have come to work with me, I have found a sense of peace. I still don't know if I believe in a literal God but, if there is one, I hope that he will have mercy on me.

[The officer again raps on the window and enters. He handcuffs Bundy and leads him out of the room. When Ted reaches the door he turns back briefly as though he has more that he wants to say. He looks away from me and the door closes slowly behind him. I sit there for several minutes thinking about Ted. He is skilled and intelligent. He has charisma. What could he have accomplished for himself and for society had he not allowed himself to create a personality of a killer? Was he even aware that he was the author of his own destruction?]

Epilogue

The key to who Ted Bundy was lies in what he called the Entity. He wasn't talking about a spirit or something supernatural inside of him. He was speaking of an overwhelming urge that would take control over him. While many believe that talk of an Entity was only Bundy's way of attempting to avoid responsibility for his crimes, it may be more than that. He told Stephen G. Michaud and Hugh Aynesworth about this Entity when he was talking in the third person and was still denying guilt for his crimes. There was no need to introduce the concept of another personality force into the killer's behavior if he was just gaming.

Possibly the first person to whom he mentioned this other force was his girlfriend Elizabeth "Liz" Kendall. In her book *Phantom Prince* she wrote about a conversation with him over the phone after the police picked him up:

There is something the matter with me . . . I just couldn't contain it. I've fought it for a long, long time . . . it got too strong. We just happened to be going together when it got under way. I tried, believe me, I tried to suppress it. It was taking more and more of my time. That's why I didn't do well in school. My time was being used trying to make my life look normal. But it wasn't normal. All the time I could feel that force building in me . . . [35]

Liz asked if he used her to keep in touch with reality. She referred to the night he phoned her after the DaRonch and Kent episodes. Ted said,

Yeah, that's a pretty good guess. It's like it's over. I don't have a split personality. I don't have blackouts. I remember everything I've done. Like Lake Sammamish. We went out to Farrell's for ice cream after eating hamburgers. It wasn't like I had forgotten or couldn't remember, but it was just over . . . gone . . . the force wasn't pushing me anymore. I don't understand it. The force would just consume me. Like one night I was walking by the campus and I followed this sorority girl. I didn't want to follow her. I didn't do anything but follow her and that's how it was. I'd be out late at night and follow people like that . . . I'd try not to but I'd do it anyway. [36]

Probably the last persons he talked to about the Entity were his lawyer Poly Nelson and Dr. Dorothy Lewis. He never said the Entity killed his victims but he was consistent in his statements about this entity force controlling him. Dr. Lewis, a New York psychiatrist who testified at one of Bundy's trials, said she believed that he had a bipolar disorder with multiple personality disorder traits. On the other hand, many people who have known Ted Bundy have liked him. So it is difficult to know the truth.

I don't believe that we should look upon Ted Bundy as a victim. He was a cold-blooded killer who justified his crimes by claiming it was no worse to kill a human being than to kill an elk or deer and hang the trophy head on a wall.

I do believe that Bundy likely had this process going on within him that he referred to as an Entity. To him it was something foreign, something that would get out of control and he would find himself doing things that he would seriously regret later. Ted created the Entity. He was the author of what he became and by so doing he was fully responsible for his criminal behavior.

It began with loneliness to which he responded by creating a fantasy life. He indulged in this fantasy activity whenever he was lonely, angry, or depressed. He attempted to push the limits of this fantasy process in order to turn it into reality so that he could actually sense that it was happening, and not just imagine it. In repeating this process hundreds and thousands of times, he learned to dissociate. Dissociation in this sense would be a process in which when slipping into this fantasy imagery he could block out, or gate out, everything going on around him. He could emotionally enhance it so that he would sense that he was actually there, hearing the background sounds, smelling the smells, hearing the declarations of love—or the screams.

Hero fantasies would become control fantasies which in turn would become revenge fantasies. Souvenirs would be taken in order to enhance the reliving of the crime. (Ted took the heads of victims to his apartment.) In this way, the fantasized reality could go on for hours. This could generate separate neural fibers in his brain, parallel neural pathways that when stimulated would set into action a series of behaviors that would follow a given sequence until the act was completed. In Bundy's case, the end result often seemed not to be the killing of the victim, but in the fantasy love action that followed.

Was Ted the only person who has ever developed this internal process? I don't think so. I believe it is likely going on within some now and we will see it happen again in the future. Not all who engage in intense pathological fantasy will kill, but some may.

Who will be next?

End Notes

1. Nelson, pp. 284-288
2. Holmes, 1998, p. 88
3. "Bill" (personal communication, 1989)
4. Michaud, 1989, p. 72
5. Michaud, p. 74
6. Michaud, p. 172
7. "Bob" (personal communication, 1984)
8. ibid
9. ibid
10. ibid
11. Bill (personal communication, 2014)
12. "Mary" (personal communication, 1975)
13. Bill (personal communication, 1989)
14. ibid

15. ibid
16. ibid
17. "Joan" (personal communication, 1975)
18. "Marjorie" (personal communication, 1975)
19. Bill (personal communication, 1989)
20. Michaud, 1989, p. 72
21. Michaud, p. 77
22. Michaud, p. 79
23. Michaud, p. 74
24. Kendall, 1981, p. 21
25. Rule, 2009, p. 22
26. Rule, p. 618
27. "Jackie" (personal communication, 1975)
28. "Sharon" (personal communication, 1975)
29. ibid
30. "Michael" (personal communication, 1975)
31. Bill (personal communication, 1989)
32. Kendall, 1981, p. 52
33. J. Thompson (personal communication, 1990)
34. Masters, 1985, pp. 241-243
35. E. Kendall (personal communication, 1975)
36. Kendall, 1981, p. 174
37. Kendall, pp. 175-176

References

DePaulo, B, Ed. (2010). *The psychology of Dexter*. Dallas, TX: BenBella.

Holmes, R. M. and S. T. Holmes, Eds. (1998). *Contemporary perspectives on serial murder*. Thousand Oaks, CA: SAGE.

Kendall, E. (1981). *The phantom prince: My life with Ted Bundy*. McMinnville, OR: Madrona.

Masters, B. (1985). *Killing for company: The case of Dennis Nilsen*. New York: Stein and Day.

Michaud, S. & Aynesworth, H. (1989). *Ted Bundy: Conversations with a killer*. New York: Signet.

Nelson, P. (1994). *Defending the devil: My story as Ted Bundy's last lawyer*. New York: William Morrow & Co.

Rule, A. (2009). *The Stranger beside me*. New York: Simon & Schuster.

Acknowledgments

When I conducted my initial evaluation of Ted Bundy for the court in 1976, I had no thought of ever writing a book. Over the years many of my colleagues, family, and friends encouraged me to put my impressions of him in print. To all of those who have given me constant encouragement and support towards this end: Thank you very much.

Special appreciation goes to my agent, Carrie Anne Keller; to my publisher, Steven W. Booth; and my editor, Leya Booth. Without their patience and encouragement this project would not have been completed. I am very grateful to Dr. Michael R. Collings for his editorial consultation as well as his positive in-spiration. I want to express my thanks to the designer of our new cover, Cyrus Wraith Walker, for his outstanding, professional work. Also, I would like to give particular thanks to Shelley

Welsh for her patient reading and re-reading of the manuscript and suggesting changes.

I want to give thanks to those who knew Ted Bundy and were willing to tell me of their experiences and their impressions of him. This applies both to those who were impressed with him and those who informed me of his dark side. I owe deep gratitude to Detective Jerry Thompson (Ret.) who doggedly pursued Ted, while other law enforcement personnel attempted to discourage him from doing so. His willingness to share his valuable insight into Ted's behavior during the investigation added another dimension to my research.

I owe my deep gratitude to the late Dick Larsen, Associate Editor of the Seattle Times, and his willingness to take a day out of his busy schedule to discuss with me his research on Bundy. An additional appreciation goes to his widow, Deanie Larsen, who allowed me to spend a couple of days reviewing Dick's research materials. Dr. Ron Holmes and the late Parole Officer Jim Massy provided valuable insights about Ted, as well.

Thanks go to authors of works on Ted who shared their insights with me. These include Dr. Ron Holmes, Kevin Sullivan, Dick Larsen, Dr. Katherine Ramsland, Hugh Aynesworth, and Stephen Michaud. A special thanks goes to Manuel Cortez and "Bill" for their insights on the violent mind and their willingness to share them with me. I want to express appreciation to the inmates at the Utah State Prison who were willing to share their stories for my research on violence.

Finally, I want to express my appreciation to my wife JoAnn and my wonderful children Charlene, Steve, Rob, and Tom for their patience and understanding during the years I spent gathering information on the violent mind.

CPSIA information can be obtained
at www.ICGtesting.com
Printed in the USA
BVHW01s0818190218
508508BV00007B/16/P